# We're Laughing With You, Not At You

## *...And Other Frightening Tales of Life*

**Matt Wixon**

"We're Laughing With You, Not At You ... And Other Frightening Tales of Life" by Matt Wixon. ISBN 1-58939-123-3.

Published 2001 by Virtualbookworm.com Publishing Inc., P.O. Box 9949, College Station, TX , 77842, US. 

Manufactured in the United States of America.

## *To Janell*

## Special Thanks to:

My family, as well as my friends at The Dallas Morning News, Yuma Daily Sun and Arizona Daily Sun

## About the Cover:

I don't know who decided I would be a witch for Halloween and my brother would be a gender-bending ballerina, but I do know that someone needed to take the lipstick away from my sister.

# Contents

# Introduction

The columns in this collection were written over a three-year period, and I thought it might take another three years to come up with a title for the book. Here's the problem: What exactly do columns about Kit Kat auditions, screaming little-league parents and swing-dancing disasters have in common?

Nothing, other than that they first appeared in my newspaper column. Considering that, maybe the best title for this book would be *Please See Jump On Page 6C*, because many of my columns jump from one page to another. At least it's better than when I was a sports columnist, and my final thoughts were typically butted up against advertisements for back-hair removal or camouflage wallets.

But I won't complain, because I am grateful for the newspapers that run my columns. And I am grateful for anyone who reads this book, which is why I wanted a really snappy title to lure in readers. My first attempt was *Ninety Ways to Solve Your Problem Thighs, Become Financially Secure and Repair Your Relationship, as seen on Oprah.* But the publisher assured me that this title would cause problems, so I took another shot at it.

That's when I came up with *We're Laughing With You, Not At You.* It's a saying that my teachers would tell students after they dropped their lunch trays, tripped on the playground, or in my case, had his fifth-grade solar-system project fall off the table and break during his presentation. My thought was, "How can you be laughing with me if I'm not laughing?"

It was one of those lies adults tell kids to make them feel better, much like "You can do anything in this world if you set your mind to it." I've been working on my basketball skills for nearly 30 years, and I still don't see any pro basketball teams calling me. Apparently, although I dreamed of being a pro basketball player, I didn't *set my mind to it*. It couldn't have anything to do with the fact that I'm too slow and can barely jump over this book.

Anyway, lies seemed to be the only common theme in this book. There aren't a lot of them, but I admit that I never listed pain and suffering as a deduction on my taxes, that I might have overestimated the amount of people at a *Wheel of Fortune* audition (a bazillion), and that I've never been mistaken for Brad Pitt. But I think most people know when I'm lying, just like everyone knows that although the photo on the back of this book makes me appear to be a youngish man, I am actually a 72-year-old woman with four children and seven grandkids. I love playing Scrabble with Ann Landers and eating Oreo cookies with my cats.

So that's how I came up with the title. I certainly hope you enjoy the book, and if you do, please buy one for a friend. If you don't enjoy it, well, let's just keep that quiet. And come by sometime and we'll talk it over. I can usually be found at *The Dallas Morning News* battling the vending machine for some Oreos.

# Showering the world with male truth

A few years ago a friend asked me for help after her car broke down. Thankfully, like all real men, I am a natural Mr. Goodwrench.

I walked around the car, surveyed the situation and gave her my assessment: "You should probably ask someone who knows something about cars."

It was another achievement in my quest to obliterate male stereotypes. Some of my other successes include failed household projects, stopping at a gas station for directions, and once, back when I was in college, refusing to give a roommate a high-five after he banked an empty Coke can off the wall and into a wastebasket.

Breaking down these stereotypes is important, so I'm happy to do my part. And one day, I expect to live in a world that is free of gender stereotypes, or at least a world where I don't have to pretend that I like Steven Seagal movies.

But redefining what a real man is can be exhausting. Sometimes, after a long day of bungling home repairs, putting the toilet seat down and failing to swig even one beer while sitting in a Barcolounger, I'm too tired to whip up a quiche and watch *Oprah*.

OK, I'm not that devoted to breaking down male stereotypes. I don't have enough energy or attraction to quiche. I also admit that I'm often tempted to give in and embrace the stereotype, or at least the low expectations that come with it.

It just seems that life would be simpler if I wasn't expected to remember my anniversary, my wife's birthday or that the trash needs to be taken out. Life would also be easier if I if could tender a gender excuse whenever I'm accused of insensitivity or an uncouth manner. And wouldn't my life be a snap if it followed the script of a beer commercial? I could dazzle all the women, many of which would be wearing bikinis, by simply ordering the right brew.

Yes, low expectations can be a man's best friend. And a few brave men are working to keep the standard low. Check out this evidence recently printed in the newspaper:

Dear Abby: My husband works in the construction trade and refuses to bathe more than once a week. Am I unreasonable to expect him to shower at least every two to three days?

Disgusting. But also amazing. Somehow this guy has set the bar so low that his wife is only requesting a shower every couple of days. I would really like to meet him, as long as it's on the one day a week he showers.

Living the stereotype is indeed tempting, as well as water conscious. But I want to be a little more in touch with my sense of responsibility.

I don't think it's just me. I think most men want to be viewed as more than hormone-driven slobs who drool over supermodels, talk endlessly about horsepower and do their Christmas shopping on December 24. We're not just stupid, boorish animals who watch sports all day; we're caring, introspective individuals who will talk about our feelings, at least during the commercials.

Eventually the stereotype will end, along with the other hurtful stereotypes in the world. But what can men do to speed up the process?

Educate.

Stop a woman on the street and tell her about your feelings. Show her a ticket stub to a movie starring Julia Roberts. Admit that when you lift your car's hood, you don't know an exhaust manifold from a pollution-control valve.

But above all, take a shower before beginning the education.

# The hottest fund-raiser: cheese, sausage and guilt

As I reached for the doorbell — my arms full of delicious ways for my neighbor to support my school — I glanced down at the fund-raising kit's suggested opening line:

"Hello, my name is (your name here) and I am selling delicious cheese-and-sausage products to raise money for (your school here)."

That opening line would work fine, but I knew it wouldn't make me the top cheese-and-sausage salesman at my school. So I decided to add in how my school needed new playground equipment and that the top salesman would win a trip to Disneyland, where I had always dreamed of visiting (insert 10-year-old grin here).

Who could resist such a dramatic presentation?

As it turned out, just about everyone. But at least they offered legitimate-sounding excuses. Some couldn't find their wallet or purse. Others had already bought cheese and sausage from another student. A few were allergic to both cheese and sausage — and talk about bad luck — they were also allergic to the pecan rolls, candy bars and caramel popcorn I was shilling.

"I also have coupon books," I would add.

"I think I hear the phone ringing," was their response, "and a pot may be boiling over on the stove."

I got the point.

At some houses, I didn't even get to make my point. As I approached the front door, the lights in the house would go out, the blinds would close and the television would become silent. I would hear faint whispers of "Be quiet!" and "Is he gone yet?"

It's hard to believe people could do that to an innocent child walking the mean streets of fund-raiser world. What's harder to believe, however, is that I've become one of those people.

How quickly I forgot my childhood dearth as a salesman. The days when neighbors became targets as I parroted my opening line and hoped that someone would buy a raffle ticket, a box of caramel delights or sponsor me in my basketball team's Hoop-a-thon. The days when my relatives had an ample supply of my car-wash coupons and nine-dollar cheese spreads.

These days, I'm the one peering through the blinds for pint-sized pitch men and pretending not to exist when they ring my doorbell. Yes, I know they're raising money for a good cause, and yes, I feel guilty. Especially when I see them walking dejectedly away from my door wearing their soccer uniforms or T-shirts with their dance team's name on the front.

How can I be so heartless?

I'm not really sure. But somewhere in the sales assault of cookies, homemade wrapping paper and Wisconsin cheddar logs, I realized there are just too many good causes and even more good "saleskids."

"Hello, my name is Michael, and I am selling candy bars for my swim team," said a recent visitor. "Do you like to swim?"

Do I like to swim? I just knew that he tacked that on to the suggested opening line. He was that good.

As he continued his pitch, I hoped that a phone would ring, a pot would boil over or an excuse better than "I'm sorry, but I'm busy making the world safe for democracy" would pop into my head.

It was too late for an excuse, anyway. Michael had rattled off his entire line of products and I felt too guilty to close the door.

With no escape, I settled on the chocolate bar with almonds, which looked a little mushy as Michael pulled it out of the box. Chocolate oozed from one end of the wrapper as I pulled two dollars from my wallet.

I paid him and he was off to his next customer. For a moment I felt the satisfaction of supporting a good cause, until my dogs began licking the chocolate dripping off my fingers. Too bad Michael didn't have any napkins.

That's the next fund-raiser, I suppose.

# Shop 'til you drop or the schoolbell rings

A mall opened near my house recently, bringing the exciting world of credit-card debt closer to my neighborhood. It's a typical mall, with anchor stores like Dillard's and Macy's, a food court dripping with grease, and teenagers with pagers making out near the ice rink. It also has specialty stores featuring indispensable products like antique Pez dispensers and "executive" back-scratchers.

What makes a back-scratcher an "executive" back-scratcher? Well, it's crafted from fine wood, has a padded handle and is the perfect gift for the executive in your life. And when you're an executive, how can you land the big promotion if the boss sees you doing something barbaric like scratching your back with your hand?

Moving from back-scratchers to head-scratchers, here's one that boggles me: The nothing-but-candles shop. That's right, a store that sells nothing but candles and candle paraphernalia.

Just how much money can you make selling candles?

A lot, apparently. My wife took me in there, probably to test how serious I was about our wedding vows, and I discovered how expensive candles can be. I had no idea anyone could charge that much for scented candles shaped like the state of Texas. I also have no idea if my wife bought any, because the potpourri pollution forced me from the store in less than five minutes. Another 10 seconds in there and I would've coughed up a dried flower.

Of course there are many other unusual stores at the mall, each one exciting enough to pack the parking lot. There's also a Starbucks on each level, which seems a little ridiculous. But I figure it's a cost-control measure. Imagine how many shoppers could lose their caffeine buzz on the escalator, and just as they are pleading for a double-delicious-mucho-mocha, collapse and wipe out an entire row of perfumed body splash at Bath and Body Works.

Even worse, the fallen shopper could mess up some meticulously folded sweaters at the Gap, which of course is in the mall because federal fashion regulations require it. The Gap is near other dangerously hip stores like J. Crew and Abercrombie & Fitch, where my neighborhood's Clearasil demographic can find trendy sweaters, happenin' pants and people to make out with by the ice rink.

As I said, the mall near me is pretty typical. But here's what makes it special: It not only has a Gap, it has Gap Kids and Baby Gap stores. That means after years of fruitless searching, a fashion-forward 3-year-old finally has a place to buy leather pants.

Yes, leather pants for toddlers. They come in lots of colors, too — to match the extensive wardrobes of modern babies. And if Baby Gap and Gap Kids isn't enough shopping for the younger set, there's also Old Navy for kids and babies, Talbot's Kids and the Cigars for Babies Store.

OK, that last one hasn't opened yet. But it will probably open soon, along with Mervyn's Baby, Tommy Hilfiger Toddler and the Nike Tike Store. They'll be somewhere near Pottery Barn Kids, a store that really does exist — and I'm sure fulfills every child's greatest wish.

"Hey Little Suzie, would you like a dolly for your birthday?"

"No, I want a Belvedere Ottoman, some Claro Stemware and a Juit and Coir Natural Fiber Rug."

Now that's the shopper of tomorrow the malls must cultivate today. And if mommy and daddy can't pay for it all right now, they can always use the easy payment plan. That way they can teach little Suzie about math while she coordinates accent colors in her bedroom.

"Hey Little Suzie, do you know what $10,000 on credit cards at 18 percent interest means?"

It means mommy and daddy's executive back-scratcher better start paying dividends pronto.

# Cobwebs are a must at office parties

Although many people choose to flaunt their worth like peacocks searching for a mate, I've decided that humility is for me. It just seems more dignified and appropriate to keep my stunning good looks, abundant intelligence and sparkling personality to myself. And I'm sure my personal assistant would agree, but right now he's out picking up the wall-sized oil painting of me standing in front of my BMW.

So please bear with me today as I step from my humble shoes and proclaim that I know more about this week's weather than anybody. I'm also ready to claim the top prize on *Who Wants to Be a Millionaire* if the questions involve any of the following topics: The kind of cheese in the mini quiches, whether it is too hot in the room, what I do for a living, the beautiful decorations on the Christmas tree, and a cobweb dangling from the ceiling above the Christmas tree.

At this point in the column, I'm probably obligated to tell you what I'm writing about. Let me just say this: The column would make a lot more sense if you were drinking eggnog with me.

Just kidding, of course. The real reason I know so much about nothing right now, in addition to my degree in journalism, is that I attended my wife's office holiday party last weekend. It was a festive collection of teachers and staff from her school, and the party was filled with music, games, food and long, uncomfortable conversations that were dead on arrival.

"The weather is getting colder," one man said to me, breaking the ice and finding a topic that would eat up at least thirty seconds of the three-hour party.

"Yes, it certainly is," I said, wishing I had more to offer.

"The weatherman said it's a cold front coming through," he

added.

"Really? That's certainly interesting," I said, in a lie nearly as big as the extracurricular activities I listed on my college applications.

"The decorations on the Christmas tree are also very nice," he said, scurrying for another available topic.

"They certainly are," I said, realizing that I wasn't helping the conversation and, more important, that I use the word "certainly" way too much.

That was it. We were out of things to say. So we did what everyone does when conversations go belly up — we started scanning the room. That's when I noticed the cobweb near the ceiling above the Christmas tree. It would become one of my focal points for the evening as I walked around the room with an interested look.

What is the interested look?

The interested look is a great strategy for uncomfortable social situations. It keeps people from talking to you because you appear content looking at the mini quiches, rattling ice in your cup or reading the container for the toothpicks. "WARNING: Do not put toothpicks in ear." Yes, that's a good tip, and a reason to give an interested look.

My only other strategy for awkward social situations is to fake a migraine and then faint. But you can only use that one once.

So Saturday night I had to stay conscious, which was difficult at times. I joined in certified time-killer conversations about plastic forks, ice cubes, salad dressing, and of course, the impending cold front of doom that just couldn't be analyzed enough. And when the conversation ran dry, I turned my head, scanned the room and checked on the cobweb.

How long could it dangle? Would it make it the entire night? How long could the cobweb drama go on?

I was hoping about three hours. Or at least until my wife asked me if I had a migraine.

# Life, liberty and the pursuit of parking spaces

Another Thanksgiving is here, a time to take a break from life's hectic pace, give thanks for all that we have and plan strategy for the busiest shopping day of the year. I'll be at the mall tomorrow, too, sitting in my car in a parking spot counting how many people ask me when I'm going to leave.

That's for the day after Thanksgiving, but today, I'm counting my blessings. For example, I'm thankful that this is not a sports column, and therefore won't be butted up against an advertisement for back-hair removal. And the sports editor can't tell me to cut a few paragraphs because the paper sold a bigger ad for camouflage air rifles.

Of course, I'm thankful for much greater things: my wife, my family, my health, the shrinking amount of hair that remains loyal to the top of my head. I'm also thankful for the country in which I live. To be sure of it, I did a manual recount of my vote, and NBC, ABC, CBS, Fox and CNN are now reporting that I am thankful for this country.

I'm thankful for this country because of the opportunities it offered me. From the day I started elementary school, I knew that if I paid attention to the teachers, did all my assignments and tried to do my best, at some point I would be stuffed into a trash can during recess. But I also knew that I would learn a lot in school, like the story of the original Thanksgiving.

Many people believe the first Thanksgiving never happened. That might be true, but maybe those people are cynical because they were duped by Milli Vanilli. You know, fool me once, shame on you, fool me twice, shame on me.

But as the story goes, Thanksgiving began when the pilgrims

and indians shared a feast sometime between the Franco-American War and the War of the Worlds. It was an important event because the pilgrims and indians sat down together to share a meal, exchange ideas and place bets on the Vikings-Lions game. Records indicate the whole day was sponsored by Miller Lite, and in a move to ensure a lasting peace, the pilgrims and indians agreed that the beer both tasted great *and* was less filling.

Many Thanksgivings have passed since then, but the ideal has not. In this country, we still have the right to life, liberty and the pursuit of as many cable channels as possible, including the 24-hour wicker crafts network.

And if we're not into the wicker channel, we are free to use the remote.

After all, freedom is what makes this country great. We have freedom of religion, freedom of expression and the freedom from high interest rates with the new Chuck's Corner Store Platinum credit card. We have free elections, a free market and a free football phone when we sign up for 52 issues of some magazine at 60 percent off the newsstand price.

And no other country can match our rights. We have the right to bear arms and arm ourselves with the latest breakthrough in vegetable slicers. We have the right to a phone call when arrested and the right to save money by dialing 1-800 COLLECT. We have the right to a trial by jury and a free trial offer from the leader in fat-blasting technology.

What a country, and what great reasons to be thankful. So before we plunge into the monthlong hysteria of Christmas, remember that today is for peace, understanding and counting our blessings.

Happy Thanksgiving. Tomorrow my parking spot costs 20 bucks.

# The best gift for an 8-year-old is not ...

Standing on the patio waiting for my turn to pin the tail on the donkey, my 8-year-old mind counted down to disaster. Each second ticked louder as I waited for the humiliation bomb to explode and doom me to a life inside my bedroom.

They would all laugh, that I knew. But would the events of the birthday party get back to my school? I cringed at the thought of such delicate information making its way into the hands of the third grade's Powers That Be. The powers that had the ability to turn molehills into mountains, Cooties into a devastating social disease, and one kid's upset stomach into a nickname he would never escape: Barfy.

It had all happened so fast, the birthday-party reversal of fortune. One moment I was looking forward to my friend Lance's party; the next I was longing for an abandoned refrigerator I could climb into. I got more nervous as the moment of my demise grew near. The ticking got louder, and I nearly missed the entire donkey, pinning the tail between its ears.

As we started another birthday game, I wondered if the other kids knew something was wrong. Sure, I looked cool. In fact, I felt like the height of late '70s fashion. I had the Ocean Pacific-brand corduroy shorts on and my favorite tube socks, the ones with the green stripes, pulled up to my knees. But the ticking grew louder, and I swore they knew. In the balloon relay, a birthday-party sport I normally excelled in, I couldn't even pop one.

I had to do something.

"I hope you get some good stuff for your birthday," I said to Lance, "and I hope you get something good from me, too. I really don't know what I got you. My mom got it."

Playing dumb was my only hope. I had to lay the groundwork for more excuses to come.

"Yeah, she got the gift for you when I was at school," I said to Lance, as we shared some of the birthday cake, and hopefully the understanding that I was not involved in the selection of the gift. "I told her to get you that new Atari game."

An Atari game would've been a hit. Anything electronic that made beeping noises would've been fine. Or how about a Star Wars action figure? Lance and I were a little beyond that age, but it still could pass without notice, without the uproarious laughter that was sure to come when Lance opened my gift. For a moment, I thought that even something from the Barbie collection would be better than my offering.

But I wasn't that lucky. And I shivered as Lance's mother announced it was time to open the gifts.

Lance got the Atari game. He also got several electronic games that made lots of beeping noises. He even got a Star Wars action figure, which he rolled his eyes at. And then ...

"This one is from Matt," Lance's mother said.

Ticktock. Kaboom.

"What is it?" Lance asked, pulling the last bits of wrapping paper off. I shrugged my shoulders, playing the naive strategy into overtime.

"It's a pair of moccasins," Lance's mom said, serving as the opening bell to a four-alarm blaze of laughter.

The laughter started in the front of the room and quickly spread to the back. It raged all around me. Where was an abandoned refrigerator when you needed it?

Lance's mother tried to help: "Matt, the kids are laughing with you, not at you."

Of course, I knew that was a lie. I always know when people are laughing at me, not with me. And two weeks later, when I returned to the scene of the moccasin drama, I knew I was laughing at Lance, not with him.

His mom made him wear them.

# Stay sweet, show spirit and K.I.T.

In response to the accusations that my claims are fraudulent, I present this irrefutable evidence that I was one very cool dude in high school:

(From Page 227 of the 1989 Apollo Yearbook, "Splash of Spirit")

"Matt you are the coolest. You rock!"

There you have it. And that note in my yearbook wasn't written by just anyone. On the recommendation of my lawyer, I am not revealing his name, but he was a bona fide member of the "A" crowd at Apollo High. This guy was in the Chess Club, the Science Fiction Club and even played trombone in the band!

Yes, it's a great self-esteem boost looking through that yearbook, even if strands of my hair fall onto the pages as I read them. It takes me back to my high school days, when I had lots of hair and lots of people who looked to me for direction, especially in math class.

(From Page 62)

"Matt, you are the best! Thanks for all the answers you gave me in precalculus class."

The rest of the yearbook isn't as great. In fact, some might get the idea that I was not extremely popular in high school. For example, I'm not in any of the photos scattered throughout the yearbook. I'm only in the class pictures section, ranking my yearbook presence just above the classmates with PICTURE NOT AVAILABLE where a face should be.

But it's a typical yearbook, so the photo packages like "Hawks show spirit by giving blood," "Hawks' spirit shows at pep rallies," and "Hawks get into Homecoming spirit" feature the same people over and over. Even in the organizations sections — which feature clever headlines like "Computer students log on" and "Home economics really cooks this year" — I've noticed that most of the photos are of the yearbook staff, friends of the yearbook staff, and of people making silly faces while wearing Bon Jovi T-shirts.

That just wasn't my style. I swam far from the mainstream, as most cool people do, even rebelling against those cliché high school parties by staying home and watching television on Saturday nights. And you know, "Student shows Hawk spirit by watching *Miami Vice* on videotape" never ends up in the yearbook.

I lived by my own rules in those freewheeling days of adolescence, which made me a somewhat misunderstood, yet very popular, member of the Class of 1989. Maybe it was my uniquely secluded personality that made me so revered in high school. More evidence:

(From Page 239)

"Matt, it was nice talking to you that one time."

"Matt, it was great being in English class with you. You were in the class, right?"

"Mark, best of luck in the future. Maybe I'll see you."

Obviously there was some confusion about my name on that last one, but there can be no doubting my popularity. And here's a final bit of evidence:

(From Page 240)

"Matt, have a nice life."

That last note is particularly juicy because it came from a girl. That's no surprise, however, because I was very popular with the girls. None of them actually went out on a date with me, but I'm guessing that's because they were intimidated. I bet they were frightened that my standards would be way too high for them to be acceptable.

Of course my standards weren't that high, but when you're 17 years old, you don't always think clearly. That's obvious in the Top 15 News Items of the 1988-89 school year, as voted on by Apollo students. Number 13 is *E.T.* comes out on videocassette.

Maybe that cloudy thinking is why so many of my classmates ended notes in my yearbook with K.I.T. (teenage shorthand for Keep In Touch), but forgot to leave their phone number.

I'm sure they are waiting to hear from me.

# Hey waiter, hold the 'Happy Birthday!'

Restaurant reviews go into great detail about the food, service, and of course the ambiance, commonly referred to as "something you rarely find at Kentucky Fried Chicken."

But what is ambiance, other than an excellent word for thinning out spelling bees? Well, Merriam-Webster's Dictionary defines it as "a feeling or mood associated with a particular place, person, or thing." But the best way to understand ambiance — at least restaurant ambiance, anyway — is through comparison:

**GOOD AMBIANCE:** Comfortable room temperature, pleasant décor and the waiters are friendly.

**BAD AMBIANCE:** Comfortable room temperature, pleasant décor, and every 10 minutes the complete serving staff trots out of the kitchen, puts on silly grins and sings "Happy, Happy Birthday" to some poor soul.

Actually, the first "Happy, Happy Birthday" of the night might qualify as good ambiance. It's part of the restaurant's relaxed, fun atmosphere, which many people like because they can wear shorts and won't encounter a waiter named Jean Pierre who laughs at their wine selection. And I admit that I've inflicted the "Happy, Happy Birthday" song, which has many variations at many different restaurants, on one of my friends. After I told the server of the birthday, my friend swore revenge for having to eat his bacon cheeseburger with a balloon tied to his arm.

But it was fun, which is usually the case for the first "Happy, Happy Birthday" of the night. I can even handle two. It is casual dining, after all, and a double dose of "Happy, Happy Birthday" is worth not having to worry about whether chicken fingers demand Cabernet Sauvignon or Zinfandel.

But the evening's third "Happy, Happy Birthday" is rarely a happy, happy thing. And a fourth chorus begs the question, "Have these birthdays been verified?"

I wanted to ask that question to Jason, who served my table during a recent night of happy, happy birthdays. Despite wearing a funny hat and describing most menu items as "deliciously awesome," Jason appeared to take his job seriously. The problem was, he rarely appeared, except to join in seven, yes seven, "Happy, Happy Birthdays."

*"Happy, happy birthday,*
*this is your special day,*
*we hope that you enjoy it,*
*in every single way, hey!"*

Seven in less than one hour. That's a lot of happy, happy birthdays. And it's probably why there were lots of empty, empty glasses waiting for refills.

But I couldn't blame Jason, who was struggling to balance his duties as fajita courier and singing telegram. It can't be easy to belt out the "Happy, Happy Birthday" song while trying to remember that Table 17 wants extra onions on a quesadilla and Table 12 wants less ice in a sarsaparilla. And how can you hit all the tables for refills when you're counted on to hit high notes?

That was another question for Jason, but he was busy. Another happy, happy birthday had begun. Hands clapped, feet stomped and conversations were put on hold like a sitcom's season-ending cliffhanger.

Jason was in the middle of it all, this time plopping a party hat on the birthday victim as she tried to hide her face from the parade of noise. But there was no escape. Jason even tied a balloon on the back of her chair, and in doing so turned toward me. His face, although partly obscured by a festive jester's cap, made him look like an actor in an Excedrin commercial. I could tell the "Happy, Happy Birthday" song was not one of Jason's favorites. Definitely not "deliciously awesome."

But I hope Jason took comfort in knowing that he helped created a special ambiance for the seven people celebrating birthdays. A server serenade, combined with friends laughing and pointing, made for birthdays so happy-happy that many honorees were speechless.

Either that or they were silently planning retribution.

# Modern life needs 'Hee Haw'

Growing up, there was something oddly reassuring about the show *Hee Haw*. I admit the emphasis here is on "oddly," considering *Hee Haw*'s 25-year run set a standard for corny jokes, terrible acting and characters in overalls that will, thankfully, never be duplicated.

But *Hee Haw* gave order to my childhood world in Phoenix. It aired each Sunday after the NFL and NBA games, and when the opening theme began, I knew the weekend was ending. I knew it was time to finish my homework and prepare for another week at Horizon Elementary — home of the Fighting Panthers and disappointing test scores.

That was in the days before cable television and satellite dishes ruled our world, so it wasn't hard to tear myself from the television. We only had five channels, and one was pickin' and grinnin' for an entire hour on Sunday nights. Other than *Hee Haw*, the choices were *M*A*S*H* reruns, the local news and *60 Minutes*, which was a shade too complicated for my Atari brain. The remaining channel was PBS, which typically filled Sunday evenings with a marathon of quality programming that included Sally Struthers or Hal Linden asking viewers to pledge $100 and receive a free tote bag.

In short, the television weekend was over for anyone under the age of 12.

These days, however, the television weekend never ends. I have a satellite dish with hundreds of channels, a total that is close to the number of tasks that remain on my chore list. I haven't crossed off many tasks lately because my time to do them keeps crossing paths with television extravaganzas like "Shark Week" on The Discovery Channel and "Beware! Bad Drivers" on The Learning Channel.

Actually, very little that I watch qualifies as an extravaganza. And although I have an extravaganza of channels, I don't watch very many of them. I watch the big networks (ABC, CBS, NBC, Fox) and a few others. I check in on MTV periodically, but that's just to confirm that I've lost radio contact with pop culture.

I also see a lot of channels accidentally when I enter the wrong number on my remote. This is easy to do because the network channels I knew growing up — Channel 3 for ABC, Channel 10 for CBS and Channel 12 for NBC — are channels 713, 738 and 763 in my satellite-dish world.

Last week my bumbling fingers led me to HBO's Spanish channel, which was airing a movie starring Mary-Kate and Ashley Olsen, the twins who have been nauseatingly lovable since before *Hee Haw* got the heave ho. I ended up watching for 30 minutes, mesmerized by Mary-Kate and Ashley's dubbed voices, which made them sound like they were 40 years old. Somehow I couldn't look away, like when passing a car accident on the freeway or watching the lady with the green eye shadow on The Home Shopping Network.

I knew I had to do something.

Give up television? I'm not that brave. That would be like my failed caffeine-free experiment, where after two days I thought I might assault a soda machine.

But I am giving up most of my channels. Too many choices takes up too much time, even if the guy who installed my satellite dish told me that only a dish would allow me to "maximize my entertainment opportunities."

He may be right. But I also remember what he said when he handed me my new remote control:

"This remote will work from anywhere in the house. If you're in the bathroom, you can still change the television in the living room."

Changing TV channels while in the bathroom. If I'm doing that, I'm halfway down a slippery slope that bottoms out with reruns of *Family Feud* and Thighmaster infomercials.

Before I fall into the abyss, I think I'll just hum the opening theme of *Hee Haw* and head to the library.

# Welcome to the family, Employee 4725A-2TI

Congratulations on landing your dream job. You'll tackle new challenges, pursue higher goals and cash a check big enough to make super-sizing your value meal a no-brainer. Make sure to focus on that your first day, when you get locked in a stairwell looking for the restroom.

The second day will be better. But the first day is like transferring to a new school, where the other children stare, nobody sits with you at lunch, and you get stuffed in a trash can during recess. Thank goodness that won't happen at work. The people are more mature and the trash cans are way too small.

More important, unprofessional behavior is prohibited by companies. It's right there in your employee handbook.

But you didn't read the employee handbook, right? Hey hot shot, don't you know how much critical information is in that handbook? Are you trying to climb the corporate ladder without a harness? Are you worried that the handbook will be like the others you've read, which failed to reach the literary heights of the instruction manual to George Foreman's Lean Mean Grilling Machine?

OK, I haven't exactly read my employee handbooks from front to back, either. But employee handbooks are obviously important. They are a "Guidebook to the Company," a "Passport to Employee Success" and a "Welcome to the Family." At least that's what my previous employers titled theirs.

Each one was like a big ol' corporate hug, assuring me that I was joining a company that cared, wanted its people to succeed and dealt seriously with the theft of office post-it notes. There were key points about vacation days, e-mail policy and parking rules, but mainly it was chummy. My "Welcome to the Family" handbook actually read like it was from the parents on *The Brady Bunch*: "We want you to be happy and succeed, so we will meet with you once a year to get your feedback, evaluate your performance and discuss your future." I'm just glad I left the company before it wanted to have the birds-and-the-bees talk.

The employee handbooks may be valuable, but they're not survival guides. What we need is a real-life guide to worklife, which I'm putting together now. It's called *You Can't Park There, Employee 4725A-2TI* and is open to suggestions. It will be full of tips that you won't find in an average employee handbook.

For example, I have never seen a handbook that points out how to deal with a vending machine that steals your money. A lot of people I know stick post-it notes, *company-owned* post-it notes, on the vending machine that read: "Owes Dave 75 cents." But the correct action is to apply the post-it note, wait for your co-workers to walk around the corner, and then kick the vending machine. If you can't get your Snickers, a kick really satisfies.

I've also never seen an employee handbook that tells you what co-workers to avoid. The answer, which probably seems obvious to those who are more workplace-savvy than me, is people who hum "Take This Job and Shove It" and want to add you to their e-mail list. Other people to avoid include those who hold daily slide-show presentations of their children or laugh loudly at their computers until you are forced to ask "What's so funny?"

And the most important workplace tip I've learned over the past 10 years, especially because I am schmooze-challenged, is to carry papers when walking down a hallway where you have to pass many people. That gives you something to look at so you can avoid eye contact and not screw up simple exchanges like ...

Co-worker: How's it going?

Me: Not much.

Dang, I swore he was going to ask me "What's going on?" Now he truly thinks I'm an idiot.

I'm just glad he didn't see me locked in the stairwell.

# Car shopping? Bring your own hot dogs

In the world of sports, good defense wins championships. In the world of car dealerships, it saves the hot dogs.

Good defense saves the hot dogs *and* the Pepsi, if the car salesmen are as good as the ones I recently had the privilege of watching.

Here's the setting: I hear a car dealership's radio advertisement, which announces that for the 47th straight week, the dealership has totally screwed up, has way too many cars and will accept any reasonable offer. And like any effective car ad, it's louder than a World Wrestling Federation introduction, says prices are so low they are insane, and the final seconds of the commercial feature a speed-talker in overdrive:

"Somerestrictionsmayapplyavailableonlyonaprovedcreditwedecidewhatisareasonableofferuseonlyasdirected."

Also mentioned in the ad were free hot dogs and Pepsi, and that perked up my ears. "Free" usually gets my attention because I am the product of an upbringing that embraced frugality like Al Gore's liplock on Tipper at the Democratic National Convention.

So I thought I would stop by, have some lunch and check out the insane prices. And sure enough, I could see smoke from a grill rising above the giant inflatable gorilla in the parking lot. Either that or it was smoke coming from the grill of my car, and in either case, it made sense to pull into the dealership.

That's when I was introduced to an elite crew of grill defenders. I wouldn't be having lunch. These guys would be having *me* for lunch.

"So what kind of vehicle are you looking for today?" asked Mike, obviously the point man for the zone defense the five customer-care representatives were playing.

"I'm just looking right now, but I plan on buying a car soon," I said, trying not to give Mike reason to further the line of questioning, but making sure he knew that I hadn't come to the lot just for a free hot dog and Pepsi. And considering someday I will buy another car, a hot dog and Pepsi weren't the only reasons I went to the dealership. I was doing research on makes, models and factory incentives. Plus, I thought they also might have cookies.

I started wandering toward the smoky goodness in the back part of the lot, but Mike wasn't letting go that easy. He began running down the standard features on one car:

"Power locks, power windows, air conditioning ..."

These features were all listed on the window sticker, so I guess Mike pegged me as illiterate.

"Cruise control, AM/FM cassette, steering column ..."

"Steering column" caught my attention. The steering column is a feature? Is there actually a base model that does not have a steering column? When you want to turn, does everyone have to lean to one side?

These were all good questions for Mike, but the only question I wanted to ask was, "Where is the relish?"

I decided to leave Mike in the dust, using the speed that in junior high earned me seventh runner-up in a sprint with eight contestants. But suddenly, a second customer-care representative was steering me away from hot-dog heaven.

"Interested in an SUVA?" he asked.

"Ugh..." I stammered, wondering where this guy came from. He must have been an athlete the caliber of Deign Sanders, who can outrun everyone in the NFL despite wearing eight pounds of jewelry.

I was in over my head. The defense was working the way it was drawn up in the showroom. I knew if I stayed another five minutes, I might be stuck in Mike's cubicle getting the tag-team hard sell on cars with prices so insane that they can't possibly let the car go without adding on a destination fee, handling fee, dealer fee, steering-column fee and ...

"severalotherfeesnotmentionedpleasesignhere."

I retreated for my old car, noticing now that the only people near the grill were car salesmen. These guys were good. So good, in fact, that they managed to hand me a stack of business cards and brochures as I steered my way around the giant inflatable gorilla.

In my rear-view mirror, I saw the longing of parents watching their child leave for college as I drove out of the parking lot as an unfinished sale.

Then Mike took a big bite of a hot dog.

# Gratuity confusion? Here's a tip

There was no way to miss it. Next to the sign for the $4.99 lunch special at the bagel shop was a big glass jar with this note posted on it: "TIPS! THANK YOU!"

The cashier saw me looking at the tip jar, and I looked back at her. Then I looked at what she had given me — a perfectly executed turkey on wheat, with neatly stacked lettuce and tomatoes. It even had the right amount of mustard. I could tell she took pride in her work, so I dug deep in my pocket, fished through some change ...

And then pulled out my car keys and drove home. I just couldn't leave a tip for a turkey bagel.

It may sound heartless, but I've got to draw the line somewhere. These days everyone wants a tip, and the sandwich artist can't compete with the other suitors of my 15 percent gratuity, like waiters, barbers and the garbage collector.

That's right, garbage collectors are supposed to get a tip. That's according to many tipping guides, which I assume were written by garbage collectors, or possibly by sports arena ushers. Ushers are also supposed to get tips, if you have enough money left after you spend $15 for a hot dog, nachos and a soda. Given the rising cost of food at sporting events, I assume the ushers take credit cards.

Dog grommets are also supposed to get tips, as are disc jockeys at nightclubs. And so should postmen, who according to tipping etiquette should get their tips in a yearly lump sum. I think the postman's tip is more like a bribe, because we all need our mail and postal workers have a history of grabbing weapons and taking their mood swings to an NBC Special Report level.

Actually, tipping and bribery are the same thing. We pay off waiters so our food doesn't accidentally get unusual ingredients in it.

We pay off skycaps so our luggage doesn't accidentally end up doing loops at a baggage claim in Cairo. We pay off parking attendants so our cars don't accidentally get sold for parts.

And we must pay off haircuts, because with a sharp pair of scissors they can either be our guide to fashionable coifs or life with one ear. That's why they are never supposed to get a tip lower than two dollars. This again is according to the helpful tipping guide, which I now believe was written by a garbage collector, arena usher and stylist at Supersets.

Two dollars seems like a big tip for the time they spend on my hair, which only required 15 minutes in my prime and gets shorter each haircut. However, I'll agree to the two-dollar tip if the haircuts agree to expand the selection of magazines in their waiting area. I'm always stuck reading teen magazines, which regularly use the words "babble" and "hunks" in the same sentence.

But the big question is, who really deserves a tip?

Teachers who take better care of their students than their parents deserve a tip. Doctors who take extra time to answer their patients' questions deserve a tip. So do all of the people who have tried to make the world a better place by volunteering their time, helping those in need or devising a plan to lock Howard Stern in a soundproof booth.

And anyone who is over 6-feet tall knows another group that deserves a tip — fast-food workers. People tall enough to see the fast-food cash registers know they have more warnings and reminders than a box of rat poison.

Did you welcome the customer? Did you ask if they wanted to Suppressive their order? Did you ask if they would like to try a new value meal? Did you ask if they want a delicious new Mr. Freeze?

Eventually, the cashier will just hand a piece of paper to the boss that says, "Did you know I'm quitting today?"

Yes, they deserve a tip. And one of these days I'm going to write a tipping guide that gives the burger-flippers their proper returns. The guide will also mention an easy way to tip the garbage collector.

Tell him he can keep 15 percent of the garbage for himself.

# Break me off some Kit Kat bravery

Just about everyone regrets a time when they played it safe in life. The time they didn't pursue the exciting, but risky, career. The time they didn't ask out the cute girl or hunk guy. The time they decided not to sing the Kit At "Gimp a Break" song at a commercial audition.

Actually, that last "they" should be an "I." It was I who turned down a brush with fame that may have rivaled my friend's appearance on *The Price is Right*, where he won a set of bedroom furniture for identifying that Downy fabric softener cost more than Bounce dryer sheets.

His price was right in 1991, and I thought my timing was right in 1996. That's when Kit At filmed a commercial at the *Arizona Daily Sun*, where I was a sports writer. The premise of the commercial was to show journalists hard at work until they stopped to enjoy some "enticing chocolate fingers," as Nestle refers to Kit Cats.

The best part: employees of the newspaper, not actors, would be the stars of the commercial.

The newsreel was buzzing when the casting crew began taking Polaroid's of potential Kit At stars. I grinned for the camera in my typically unphotogenic way, yet in a way that I thought reflected, "I am every man, and I will sell your Kit Kats."

The next day I was asked to audition. Actually, pretty much everyone was asked, but I felt special enough to entertain some ridiculous thoughts.

What if I'm so good in the commercial that Kit Kat hires me for another one? Could a commanding Kit Kat performance earn me more acting work? Would I someday be McChicken Eater No. 2 in a McDonald's commercial, or describe, in great detail, how Snickers really satisfies?

I was out of control. But my acting fantasy didn't last long. It was over as soon as I learned what I would be doing in the audition.

"We'll just ask you to sing the Kit Kat song and dance a little," the Kit Kat representative said.

Sing and dance? Somehow I thought this commercial would be different than the other Kit Kat ads. I thought it would be different because, of all the strange things I have seen in a newsroom, I have never witnessed a reporter dancing with a Kit Kat. A reporter banging on a vending machine that wouldn't drop a Kit Kat, yes. A reporter busting out some Sammy Davis Jr. moves, even for some "enticing chocolatey fingers" — never.

So I turned down the audition. And I was pretty comfortable with my decision until the day of taping. On that day, the stars of the commercial got the royal treatment. They grazed at a buffet set up for them. They sat in special chairs where crew members briefed them between takes. They were pampered and powdered while the rest of us — the newspaper employees either unwilling or unable to pull off the Kit Kat shuffle-and-sing — watched in amazement.

One of the stars was a fellow sports writer. His hair was perfect, his clothes dynamite. He looked nothing like a day earlier, when he covered a college basketball game with a huge ketchup stain on his shirt. And he was wearing so much makeup, I thought he had already been signed to do a Maybelline ad after his Kit Kat duties.

Still, I was jealous as I saw, for the first and only time, a reporter dance around a newsroom with a Kit Kat.

"Gimme a break ... gimme a break ... break me off a piece of that Kit Kat bar!" my friend sang, dancing much like Sammy Davis Jr. — if Sammy had put his shoes on the wrong feet.

My friend sure looked stupid, but I sure felt stupid for passing up the chance to look the same. Maybe it was because, even if he looked like an idiot, he was brave enough to accept the challenge. Maybe it was because the Kit Kat commercial was a sensational show-and-tell for his children. Maybe it was because the commercial aired for a year, and my friend was more than willing to tell me about the royalty checks.

I think the main reason I felt stupid was my cowardice. When I had a chance to step into the spotlight, fear kept me in the dark. I played it safe and missed an opportunity that I'm sure I will never have again.

As it turns out, enticing chocolatey fingers don't come around often in life.

# If memory serves, it doesn't serve me well

It seemed like just another day at my high school in 1985. Girls dressed like Madonna were drawing hearts on their shoes with felt-tip pens, guys wearing ripped Megadeth T-shirts were arguing over whose stereo pounded more bass, and someone had squirted ketchup all over the school's billboard — the one that said "Pride-Class-Dignity."

Yes, it was a typical day at Apollo High School in Glendale, Arizona. I had no idea that my life would change forever on that day.

That was the day I learned about simple machines, like inclined planes, pulleys and levers, in my freshman science class. That was the day the teacher used a little tune to help us remember them. That was the day I lost some of my sanity.

Let's just say the tune worked very, very well. I knew it for the test, and I knew it last night when I was trying to fall asleep. I knew it minutes before I was going to get married, and when a guy asked me for some help last week, yes sir, I knew it.

"The mechanical advantage of a simple machine is equal to that factor by which the machine multiplies the effort force," I told him.

Too bad he was asking for directions to the Holiday Inn.

Remembering the mechanical advantage of a simple machine wouldn't be so bad if not for another fact I learned in high school: Humans only use about 15 percent of their brains. So while I use only 15 percent of my brain — and it might not be that efficient because I haven't had a tuneup in years — part of that 15 percent is a holding bin for the mechanical advantage of a simple machine.

That must be why I couldn't remember where I put my sunglasses this morning. The mechanical advantage of a simple machine had encroached on the spot of my brain devoted to remembering where I put them. So less than an hour after I had last seen the glasses, I had no idea where they were. Thankfully, they were on my head.

Also taking up valuable brain space is my locker combination from high school, 27-37-6. This actually doesn't surprise me, because I had about 14 mnemonic devices to remember it. I did this out of self-preservation, because I knew when I started high school that freshmen who fumbled with their locker combinations were prime targets of the seniors, who loved to throw freshmen in trash cans or stuff them in lockers. I didn't find out until later that seniors wouldn't actually do this to me. It was mainly sophomores and juniors.

The locker combination served me well then, but I would love to delete it off my cranial hard drive now. I would also delete my high school student identification number, the preamble to the Constitution, selected verses from *Sir Gawain and the Green Knight* and the words to Cyndi Lauper's "Girls Just Wanna Have Fun." Those bits of information jumble my mind the way messages that say "Do you want to be independently wealthy?" jumble my e-mail.

And there's much more. How to say "Good morning, I'd like an egg" in German...DELETE. Two all beef patties, special sauce, lettuce, cheese, pickles, onions on a sesame seed bun...DELETE. The quadratic formula from trigonometry class — negative b plus or minus radical b squared minus 4ac all over 2a...DELETE. Here's the story, of a lovely lady...DELETE. A three-hour tour, a three-hour tour...DELETE.

Who knows what I might remember if I had all that extra space. Maybe I would remember my phone number when I tried to call home from work. Maybe I would remember to take my Big Gulp off the top of the car before I drove away from the 7-Eleven.

Maybe I would remember why I squirted ketchup all over the Apollo billboard.

# Respect for teachers is in the cards

After reading the latest report on the shortage of qualified teachers, I've decided it's time for a drastic step:

We need to put teachers on trading cards.

Yes, I'm talking about the trading cards usually associated with professional sports, and no, I haven't been drinking. I even have an idea for a commercial to run during the cartoon demographic's prime viewing times.

"Hey kids!" an excited voice will say as startling graphics bounce around the screen to poppy music, "now you can find cards of all of your favorite teachers. Collect them all!"

I know the idea sounds crazy. Teacher cards will never be coveted like cards of baseball superstars Alex Rodriguez or Ken Griffey, Jr. They won't even be as popular as cards for lesser-known major leaguers, who warm the dugout benches until there is a brawl on the mound or it's time to cash a fat check.

But trading cards might be the only way for teachers to get the respect they deserve. Imagine a card: The front features a picture of a teacher explaining a lesson, grading a paper or spending his or her lunch giving a student extra help. The back, like any good trading card, would have the pertinent statistics for the teacher:

- Made less money in 10 years than Shaquille O'Neal makes for smiling at a camera and stuffing the latest Taco Bell product in his mouth.

- Spent hours every Saturday grading papers, writing lesson plans, creating tests and buying materials for the classroom.

- After listening to people say "You're so lucky, you get your summers off," spent weekday evenings at the school's Back to School Night, Open House, Math Night, Science Night, Reading Night, Carnival Night, Parent-Teacher Conferences and McStaff Night, where teachers are asked to work at McDonald's to raise money for the school.

Maybe we can also include how many times teachers dig into their own pockets to pay for school supplies and how much they pay for their teaching licenses. And when the teacher cards are finished, we can give them some slick packaging, include a stick of gum and ...

OK, I did say it was a drastic step. But I don't see anyone following through on the other strategies for recruiting teachers. Raising salaries, improving working conditions, giving teachers more support in the classroom — for the most part it's been America's neglected homework. Our commitment to solving the teacher shortfall is like a person who vows to get fit and then bee-lines to Krispy Kreme.

So maybe it's time for teacher trading cards. Can it be any crazier than $25 million a year for a shortstop?

"Yes, it can be a lot crazier," I'm sure many people will say, including teachers. "Nobody will buy teacher trading cards."

Why not? I started my collection of baseball and basketball cards when I was 12 because I adored the players. I adored them because they did what seemed impossible. They hit 95 mph fastballs out of the park, rose like helium balloons for slam dunks and fought off hordes of tacklers for touchdowns — and still had time to do commercials for Chunky Soup.

But if you want to talk impossible tasks, try teaching a child who thinks he knows everything and believes teachers know nothing. That was me at age 13. Or try teaching an 8-year-old whose parents let him stay up late to watch *South Park*, tell him it's OK to ignore his homework and then send him to school with the idea that teachers don't deserve respect.

Don't think it happens? Ask a teacher.

"We get blamed for everything," a teacher friend of mine said.

"When test scores go down, it's the teachers' fault. Is it our fault that some parents don't care whether their child misses class or skips assignments? When kids misbehave at school and get suspended, are the parents mad at the kid? No, they're mad at the teacher or principal.

"It's our fault."

No, it's America's fault for not respecting a profession that is so important. A profession that deserves the respect given to the cover boys of the trading card world. So even if nobody will buy the teacher trading cards, I hope at least some will buy into the absurdity of the quote, "Those who can, do; those who can't, teach."

The truth is, "Those who can, do; those who can't, can always ask a teacher."

For now, that's true. But if we keep running off teachers by downplaying their importance, a teacher might not be around for help. In that case, when our children are struggling to read, write or understand math, I guess we'll have to call someone we really respect:

Our favorite major leaguer.

# This just in: Action News wins another award

Wherever you live, you should feel honored that tonight you will watch an award-winning television newscast. If you don't watch the news, and instead tune into a marathon of Richard Dawson kissing *Family Feud* contestants on the Game Show Network, it's your loss.

That's because tonight's news, brought to you by the on-the-spot eyewitness action news team in your area that really cares about you and has several cameras, will feature actual footage of news that will change your life. Either that or the weatherman will be asking 8-year-olds at the roller rink if they know about the dangers of hurricanes.

What I can tell you for sure is that the newscast will be an award-winner.

How do I know this? Is it a thorough knowledge of where all the readers of this column live? Is it a tremendous psychic ability worthy of a 30-minute infomercial with Dionne Warwick?

No. It's just that every television newscast I see brags about some kind of glorious honor it recently received. If it's not the Blue Diamond Award for Journalistic Excellence, it's the Golden Eagle Award for Integrity in Reporting or the Richard Simmons award for most chipper delivery of a story about death and destruction. There's probably even an award for best use of no video, given to the anchors of the on-the-spot eyewitness action news team that really cares about you but had a production breakdown and had to fill an entire 30-minute newscast without "going to the video."

I've seen this happen before. The poor anchor team was stuck trying to fill the show with a half-dozen stories. That newscast, which included a promo featuring the on-the-spot eyewitness action news team having a totally spontaneous, unscripted barbecue together, which of course was professionally filmed, consisted mainly of the anchors tapping their earphones and asking, "Do we have that video yet?"

The rest of the time was filled by the famous television-news banter designed to eat up time when the award-winning news team can't find any more stories to change our lives. The night of the production breakdown, I learned a lot about what the anchors were going to do that weekend. And I got a rare glimpse of a jovial weatherman pushed to the brink:

*"Hey Bob, how hot can our viewers expect it to be this weekend?"*

*"Well, it hasn't changed in the last five minutes. It's still going to be 98 degrees."*

*"OK, thanks Bob. Hey, do we have that video yet?"*

Don't get me wrong. I realize that these newscasts aren't easy to put together. And sometimes the "talent," the word used for on-air personalities, isn't all that talented. Take me, for example. I did a two-minute spot for the news in Flagstaff, Arizona, when I was a sports writer for a newspaper there. I tried to look relaxed and nonchalant, but I got nervous, started talking fast, and ended up sounding like an overcaffeinated chipmunk with an attitude. Needless to say, I wasn't asked to do a second spot. I also wasn't asked to attend the spontaneous, unscripted barbecue.

Still, I don't think the newscasts are truthful about all of their honors. I've also seen three different newscasts claim to be the fastest-growing newscast in the Southwest. I guess each has a different definition of the Southwest. One must mean the southwest portion of the Earth, while another means the southwest portion of the United States and the third means the southwest portion of the neighborhood near Sam's Gas-N-Go.

If the newscasts really are reaping all these accolades, I think it's because they congratulate themselves constantly. Each time the reporter finishes a story, the anchors assure us it was a dandy. "That was a very touching look at umbrellas," they'll say. Or my favorite: "That story is really going to help people."

I also think they're making up some awards to promote themselves, which might be a way to make this the fastest-growing column in the Southwest. So before I end this provocative, insightful, disturbing look at television news, I'd like to announce that this column has won the prestigious Shining Pen award, given for journalistic excellence in the field of trivial analysis.

That completes this column. Excellent job, Matt.

# Can I buy a vowel, or another entry?

I've always wondered what television game shows give contestants as parting gifts. A selection of Rice-A-Roni always seems to be one of them, but what else is given to the people who found their price was wrong or the wheel was of misfortune?

Well, thanks to my recent encounter with the *Wheel of Fortune*, I know of two more parting gifts. Here they are, with a few letters missing so you can play the home game:

**A sun_u_n and an in_ured t_e.**

That's right, a sunburn and an injured toe. If you guessed sunburn and an incured tie, you're the person I was hoping to face in my quest for big money.

I didn't get any money. In fact, I didn't even get on the show, so my sunburn and bruised toe may not be official parting gifts. But I was officially part of last week's *Wheel of Fortune* contestant search in Dallas.

I showed up at the megamall along with other *Wheel* watchers hoping to be *Wheel* winners. Talk about a lot of dreamers — the line stretched out the doors of the mall and a quarter mile into the parking lot. As a journalist trained to estimate the size of crowds, I would say the number was somewhere between 4,000 and a gazillion.

All for just a few slots on the show. But each of us had determined that the opportunity at big money was worth standing in the sun for an hour. Or two. Or ...

"Are you sure you want to do this?" spouses began asking their *Wheel* wannabes.

They got dirty looks in response.

I was asking myself the same thing, because my wife wouldn't. She has pushed me to go on the show for years. Both of us figured that I would go on the show, advance to the bonus round and win enough money to pay off our mortgage.

I started trying to be a *Wheel* contestant a few years ago, when the show began allowing its contestants to keep all their prize money. The original format forced players to spend their winnings on *Wheel* merchandise, which had prices more out of whack than a pair of Levi's in Russia. Remember the $400 ceramic Dalmatian?

I also remember how many times I have solved the puzzle before the contestants on the show. Yes, playing under the bright lights is different than playing at home, and maybe I would freeze up on the show. But standing in line, I kept thinking of the man who once tried to solve the puzzle "Styrofoam cup" as "Styrofoam hat."

That could be my competition.

But getting to play turned out to be much harder than any of the puzzles. Still, we were all hopeful as we dropped our entries in the big bin next to a cardboard cutout of Vanna White.

First the leaders of the audition handed out some prizes, which is when a woman's foot gave me my second parting gift. She was leaping for a *Wheel of Fortune* fanny pack and landed on my toe.

Then the auditioners drew the names of people who would play a round of the game. They said to make it to the show, we needed to be fun, enthusiastic, interesting people who spoke clearly. But clearly, most of us wouldn't get the chance to prove our *Wheel* worthiness.

I was among the rabble of disappointed. But I still have a chance, because the auditioners said they would go through the entry forms and pick a few more people in the coming weeks. And if they are looking for interesting people, they can't pass up the fabulous fiction I weaved under the question, "What are your hobbies?"

I wrote that I raise snakes and juggle knives. Shouldn't that get me on the show?

I probably have a better chance at finding big money in a Styrofoam hat.

# You're dancing on my foot, Valentine

It's almost Valentine's Day, the day when wives and girlfriends long to hear their men say those words that mean so much:

"Honey, I know I don't say this enough, but ... I saved the receipt."

Those words are a big relief for women, who can then return their special someone's romantic gift of glittering, shimmering Tupperware or the glow-in-the-dark lingerie with blinking lights, purple tassels and a nutrition label.

Sorry, wives and girlfriends. We're just not very good at Valentine's Day.

But you've known this for a long time. Back in elementary school, I remember the girls always brought in elaborate valentines that included personalized messages, candy, stickers and assorted flowers from the playground. They handed out their valentines to everyone in the class — even the weird kid — because of a teacher-imposed rule that, from personal experience, the weird kid really appreciated.

But the girls were lucky to get anything from the boys in the valentine exchange. If they did, it was because the boys' moms forced them to pick out some clever cards at the store, which featured something like a cartoon bee saying, "I'm buzzing over you, Valentine!" Boys would hand the girls the cards and say, with great sincerity, "This doesn't mean I really like you."

With such romantic roots, it's easy to understand why men have blossomed into Valentine's Day disasters.

But this year, I am the calm in the storm of battery-powered negligee, dead-in-a-week roses and heart-shaped boxes of chocolates with mystery fillings. My gift to my wife is dancing lessons for the two of us.

I should have thought of this a long time ago. I mean, what could be more romantic than getting out on the dance floor with my wife and busting out some of my newly learned Hip Hop moves? I think that would be Da Bomb. Peace to my Homies.

But this was a gift for my wife, and as it turns out, she is more interested in ballroom dancing. So we're learning how to swing dance.

We went to our first lesson last week, where we met our instructor, Mary Ellen, who I believe accidentally drank several thousand gallons of Kool-Aid before class. Either that or she's part hummingbird. She gestures wildly, taps her feet, dances around and claps her hands as she talks. I think she's the person they clone for the audiences of Ron Popeil infomercials.

Other than that, she is perfectly normal. My dancing, however, is not.

The first thing the class learned was the basic steps — slow, slow, quick, quick, slow — but the first thing I learned was that I am rhythm impaired. This is a painfully real condition, and I intend to write the government about some sort of disability payment.

While I was still trying to learn the basic steps, Mary Ellen upped the challenge. "Now we're going to add a twirl!" she said, stomping her high heels on the wood floor and speaking with excitement worthy of capital letters and five exclamation points. "THIS IS THE FUN PART!!!!!"

Well, it wasn't at first. Especially for my wife, who has the imprint of my size-13 shoe all over the top of her foot. I told her it's a beautiful momento of her husband's romantic nature.

But I am getting better, despite my disability. And I know it will all be worth it. I can see it now — the lights are low, we're dancing cheek-to-cheek, and I lean in to whisper those romantic words in her ear:

Slow, slow, quick, quick, slow.

# Nostalgia can make burnt toast perfect

Sometimes I think my mom and dad did their best parenting job on a toaster.

That's not a slap at the work they did with their human projects, who turned out fine despite being subjected to at-home haircuts during their impressionable years. It's just that my parents' toaster is 35 years old. And for most of its life, the toaster has tested parental patience like a fiercely rebellious teenager.

It has burned countless English muffins and pieces of toast. It has taken bagels and Pop Tarts hostage. And while it never threatened to dye its hair purple or get a tattoo, it was already refusing to leggo the Eggo when I was 10 years old.

"Unplug it before you stick a fork in the slots!" my mom would yell as I poked at the waffle. I'm sure she believed that I would one day become an unwitting participant in electricity research.

Twenty years later, the toaster occupies the same high-profile spot in the kitchen. My parents continue to support, nurture and encourage it. They even seem to root for it, watching intently as they drop a slice of bread into the silver abyss. Then they unplug the toaster, pull out the bread and scrape off the burnt coating.

Sometimes the toaster even refuses to take the bread. The last time I visited, my mom showed me the latest trick to making it work. "You have to bounce the bread in the slot a couple of times to get it started," she said.

I just rolled my eyes, and once again offered to buy them a new toaster. One that has wide slots, an operational lightness-darkness control and isn't a fire hazard. One that doesn't act like a 35-year-old sponging off his parents until his band gets its big break.

But my parents refuse to give up on the toaster. Maybe it's

because it was one of their wedding gifts, and they don't have many wedding mementos. Their wedding photos were stolen from their car in 1966, before cars had security systems that deterred thieves with booming alarms, imposing voices or electric shocks similar to those suffered by reckless rescuers of the Eggo.

Still, the toaster is only worth its weight on a sentimental scale. But nostalgia is powerful. It's why my dad has had the same pair of sneakers in his closet for a decade (they were partially chewed by our dog that died last year). It's why my mom still has my first pair of eyeglasses (I got them when I was 2). It's why I'm looking at the clock radio on my nightstand right now.

It's 2:36. Or it could be 2:38. The digital readout has lost a few lights over the years.

Twenty-two years, to be exact. I got the clock radio in 1979, about the same time the toaster began developing behavioral problems. Since then, the clock radio has traveled a similar dysfunctional path.

When I went to college, the digital readout began fading. Then the radio had trouble tuning in some stations. A few years ago, the choice of buzzer or wake-to-music ended when the radio opted for buzzing music as the only alarm. There were also occasions when the alarm snoozed through its wake-up duties.

And yet I couldn't get rid of it. It was my first FM radio. The radio I sat next to for hours hoping to hear Queen's "Another One Bites the Dust." The radio I held a tape recorder next to when my favorite songs were played, which made for some interesting remixes — "Jessie's Girl" with the rarely heard background vocal of "Matt, can you set the table for dinner?"

After 22 years, the radio is like a good friend. Inanimate, yes, but a good friend. So what if a few buttons don't work? I know exactly where the ones are that do work. And so what if the alarm misses a few assignments?

I think a friend knows when a friend needs more sleep.

# Memories are what you make them (up)

Life is all about losing things, a famous loser once said. OK, so I'm not famous. But I have lost a lot of things in my life, including several sets of car keys, dozens of important phone numbers and, one time on the Ripper Zipper at the Arizona State Fair, my lunch.

And this week I discovered that I've lost something else — My Hawk spirit.

Oh yeah, it's gone.

That's why it was so easy for me to turn down an invitation to my high school reunion. Sure, it would be great to reminisce with the Apollo High School Class of 1989 about the days of extra-strength Clearasil, beer bottles in the parking lot and leaving school early after bomb threats. We could also talk about braving the Marlboro smoke of the bathrooms and that time the "Skinheads" were expected to storm the campus.

And who can forget laughing at all the uncool kids in their uncool clothes? I sure can't. Because I was like, you know, for sure, totally very popular back in high school. In fact, if you bring up my name at the reunion, I'm sure the group will instantly respond with a chorus of "Who?"

Ah, memories.

But I live in Dallas now, and Phoenix is a long way from here. And buying a plane ticket, renting a black Lexus and paying a dozen or so women to scream my name as I arrive is a little pricey.

So I'm skipping the reunion. But I'll still be making a great impression. I just sent in my "Bio-Data" sheet, which will be distributed at the reunion. The sheet contains all the information on my life since graduation, and as I filled it out, I believe I reached new creative heights:

**Your occupation:** Well, being independently wealthy, I really don't have a job. But I do have several hobbies, including writing screenplays for Touchstone Pictures. I've also dabbled in television scripts, but I find that the small screen stifles my creative abilities.

**Favorite leisure activities:** With my success has come a hectic pace and finding "me" time is precious. That's why my wife and I love getting away from it all on our yacht, where I can find the solitude needed to write my autobiography, *Wonderful, Wonderful, Humble Me*.

**Favorite class in high school:** That would have to be journalism, where I learned the importance of education and the teacher let us ditch class to go to Burger King. Of course I was always ditching class, being such a rebel and all. That's why I was so popular, remember? How can you not remember? It's me, Matt — the guy with red hair.

**Favorite memory:** When everybody started chanting my name after my fifth touchdown against our archrival. Then people started bowing to me, and I thought I would just die of embarrassment. Remember how red my face was? How can you not remember? It's me, Matt — the guy with the red hair.

**Your message to the class:** Keep striving for your dreams and someday you might be like me. Never let anyone tell you that you're not good enough, remember to keep that Hawk spirit, and always cherish your high school memories.

But I'm sure you will always cherish those memories because you spent them with me, Matt.

What, you don't remember? How can you not remember?

# Class of '77 will be hard to top

Maybe I'm going to start a shouting match, but I just have to say, the Class of 1977 ruled.

A little presumptuous? Possibly.

But each member of the Kindergarten Class of '77 at Manzanita Elementary in Phoenix knew how to sit cross-legged and how to count to 10. And every one of us was educated about the deadly practice of running with scissors, as well as the use, and in some cases misuse, of paste.

We were ready for the world, or at least the first grade. So as a proud alumnus of that esteemed group, today I'm going to impart some knowledge on the world's newest students. Parents, please pass along these tips to your kindergartners, who will have a hard time reading them because — and I don't mean to brag — but I've been told I write at a third-grade level.

For openers, tears are to be expected on the first day of school, so you kids should bring some tissues for your parents. And don't worry, mom and pop will stop bawling as soon as you get in the classroom. I know, I know, parents can be so embarrassing sometimes.

Unfortunately, there will be many embarrassing moments in your life. Learning how to deal with them is an important part of kindergarten.

There will be days when classmates make fun of your name, especially if it rhymes with words like fat, cat and rat. If your name is Jamiroqoi, you're probably in the clear on this one.

But no matter what your name is, at some point you will be accused of having the Cooties. And the self-proclaimed art critic of the class will undoubtedly point out that your drawing of the dinosaur is stupid.

It can be very traumatic, so I felt I needed to warn you. And there's more. There will be times when you don't know the answer to a question, which can be really scary. But I assure you this does not mean you're dumb. That's what school is all about — learning important stuff like how Mount Rushmore is *not* a natural formation.

If you don't know that by the time you're 10 years old, it can be really embarrassing. Believe me.

But there's no reason to be scared about your voyage into the world of backpacks, recess and lining up straight. In fact, you should be excited. Starting kindergarten means you'll begin learning how to read, which is absolutely the most important part of your education.

It can be hard, but don't give up. And don't get frustrated if your first book is a little boring:

"See Spot. See Spot run. Run, run, run. See Spot run to Jane. See Jane and Spot run. Run, run, run."

I promise the books will get better. Soon you'll be reading page-turners like *Cowboy Bob's Politically Correct Simple-Sentence Adventures* and *Cowboy Bob's Multi-Syllable Roundup*. Eventually you'll get so good that you can read *Playboy* for the articles.

Just kidding. That's a lesson for a little later in life.

But now you've got all the tools for kindergarten. And you can do it. You know why? Because you're special, because you're smart and because your parents want you to succeed. They want you to get good grades, make them proud and support them when Social Security collapses. So ask them to take an active role in your learning and stress to you the importance of your education. That's their job.

Your job is to keep your hands to yourself, share your crayons and absorb information like a sponge. And remember, paste is for pasting, not tasting.

# Journalism and the art of superimposing heads

You have a degree in journalism? What exactly do you study to get that? How to chase white Ford Broncos and avoid the flying fists of Sean Penn?

I get those questions a lot, and they're just plain insulting. The truth is, classes on how to tail O.J., rummage through Madonna's dumpster and take photos of Cher's wedding — while suspended from a helicopter, of course — are just the beginning of a solid journalistic education.

I got much more than that from my journalism training at the University of Arizona (where it's officially a dirty stinking lie that Geraldo Rivera went to school there.) What my journalism education gave me was all the knowledge, expertise and skills needed to produce a newspaper, including how to superimpose the head of Elvis onto Liza Minnelli's body.

But that's only for those slow news days.

Actually, that would be a violation of journalistic ethics, which I also learned in journalism school. Now stop laughing! — that sentence is *not* supposed to be funny. It's just that some journalists don't have a tight grasp on the ethics. And us responsible types get lumped together with those jerks, who obviously skipped ethics class for the three-keg rager at Phi Delta Theta and then landed high-paying jobs at the *Weekly World News*.

Not that I am bitter.

At least my commitment to ethics has been noticed, because this week I was invited to join the Committee of Concerned Journalists. It's the most highly esteemed journalistic group I've never heard of.

Thankfully, they described themselves in the letter to me. The committee is made up of — you guessed it — concerned journalists, and their focus is "a sustained discussion of our shared principles inside newsrooms."

It doesn't sound like a real jazzy group. My guess is that many members really dig Celine Dion.

But I am thinking of joining, although I usually avoid any form of sustained discussion. I'll join because I believe it's extremely important for newspapers to improve, attract more readers and pass the benefits on to me so I can retire at age 40.

But how do we make newspapers better? Well, the newspaper can probably go no further as a window-wiper, birdcage-liner and puppy potty-trainer, so the only way to improve it is through the content. That means diving into issues that affect you. That means writing stories that move you. That means running more stories on Adam Sandler's latest movie "triumph."

Hey, it made $40 million the first weekend, so I think that's what people want.

But I'm not sure the Committee for Concerned Journalists would want that. Sandler may be a national treasure to the extra-strength Clearasil demographic group, but stories on him are "infotainment." And infotainment is a four-letter word to serious journalists, who work diligently to produce stories that most people skip to read about Prince William's new hairdo.

And even with my sterling journalism education, I'm one of those people. I can't make it more than halfway through a story about how some council is proposing a referendum to change the motion to discuss a tax on proposed referendums.

So what to do? How do we balance what some readers want, like community news, important announcements and analysis of issues, with what other readers want, like the amazing morph of Liza and Elvis?

Those are my questions for the Committee of Concerned Journalists, which will be holding a forum in the next few months to discuss topics just like that. I plan to be there, if they admit me into the group.

If they don't, I'll just hang from a helicopter and take pictures.

# Flight 1450: Something is missing in the air

Knowing that nothing in air travel is a given, including whether you'll exit the plane to a smiling "B-bye now" or as a panicked human pretzel on an inflatable slide, I guess I should've eaten the banana. But I threw it away, deciding that the breakfast bar given to me on my recent flight from Phoenix to Dallas would get me to lunch, which was to be served on my connecting flight to Philadelphia.

That's what the ticket said, anyway. And not thinking clearly, I believed it. Maybe it was because I was so busy checking on the pilot and crew, who kept assuring me that they were wide awake and their martinis were virgins. Whatever the reason, I boarded the connecting flight expecting lunch.

Yes, I was looking forward to airline food, and yes, I know that reveals my lack of culture. But I wasn't expecting filet mignon, just more than a bag of pretzels and a swig of Coke.

This is probably a good time to mention that my tale will sound like whining to any of you who, in your flight experiences, have used a seat cushion as a flotation device or have flown in a plane that became a convertible during beverage service. If either has happened to you, skip this column and proceed with your lawsuit.

Nothing that dramatic happened on my flight, for which I am truly thankful. No oxygen masks fell from the roof, no engines fell from the plane and nothing from an overhead bin fell on my head (This has happened before). But unfortunately, nothing else fell into place during the flight.

First we sat on the Dallas runway waiting for the plane to be catered. We waited for close to an hour, which in a warm, crowded plane meant our flight to Philly would be aboard a B.O. 727. At least we were waiting for food. Or so I thought.

I hoped the first round of pretzels were simply appetizers. But when the flight attendants began collecting our trash and asking if anyone wanted more pretzels, I got suspicious. So did the other passengers, who were growing surly at the thought that our one-hour sit on the runway had netted only pretzels.

"Aren't we getting lunch?" the passenger in front of me asked.

"Would you like another bag of pretzels?" the sweet-as-sugar flight attendant answered.

From that we could deduce that while American Airlines' slogan may be "Something special in the air," the something special on our flight would not be lunch. Oh, well. No big deal. The flight to Philly would be just over three hours long.

Well, that's what the ticket said.

First we circled above Philadelphia for an hour waiting to land because of bad weather. Then our captain announced that we were running out of gas and had to land in Harrisburg, where we would wait for clearance to take off for Philadelphia. Harrisburg is lovely, or at least the runway is. I got a good look at it during the two hours we sat there waiting in the plane.

Our captain kept telling us it would be just minutes before we would take off because we had "priority handling." That was no comfort, however, because my Publishers Clearing House "You May Already Be a Loser!" Sweepstakes entry is always stamped with "priority handling."

That's when that banana started sounding real good. But I figure even if I had kept it, to pull out any food at that point might have turned flight 1450 into Wrestlemania.

Eventually, as the sun was setting and just minutes before we finally took off for Philadelphia, one passenger began pleading with a flight attendant. "Since we can't get off the plane, do you have anything at all we can eat?" he said. "I haven't eaten since breakfast."

"Give me a break, sir," said the now not-so-sweet flight attendant. "I think you'll survive."

Oh, we knew we would survive. We were just wondering if the flight attendants would also make it. We had voted to eat them first.

# She's a beauty, but where are my shoes?

The brown eyes stopped me in my tracks. They were big and beautiful, and I had to take a second look. She was a knockout, no doubt. A redhead with a smile that said, "Take me home tonight."

So that's what I did. I wrote the check, opened the gate, and took home the 25-pound combination of Welsh Corgi and oversized hot dog.

I knew by her excitement as we walked to the car that I had picked the right puppy. Then, as she started to pee on the car seat, my wife and I began to realize we were actually adopting the floppy-eared spawn of Satan.

I'm kidding, of course. I do believe Satan's helpers are here on earth, but I also believe they only appear in the forms of guests on *Jerry Springer* and as overfed birds who fly above my car.

Our dog is nothing like that. She's very adorable, especially when her bladder is empty. And when we told her that it is very, very bad to pee in the car, she seemed genuinely sorry. I could tell by the look on her face that she would never, ever do it again if we never, ever let her in the car.

We named her Maggie, although she doesn't seem to know that. And I guess that's not surprising because I've observed that the wattage in Maggie's bulb is a bit low. My evidence: She often has fierce battles with her tail, is deathly afraid of water bottles and barks at the door when the phone rings.

But not knowing her name isn't all her fault, because she rarely gets called Maggie. In fact, she probably thinks her name is "No!" "Bad, Bad Dog!" or "Give me my shoe back!"

Unfortunately, Maggie has a lot of bugs in her system and she didn't come with an owner's manual or a warranty. But at least we now know the quirks of her personality, and that if anything is missing from the house, it's probably in the backyard.

That's because we have a doggie door and Maggie is a raging kleptomaniac. She tries to take everything out to the backyard, like socks, hats, pillows, the TV remote and various lamps. If the doggie door were bigger, I'd probably come home and find the dining room table getting watered with the grass.

And sitting by the wet table would be an even wetter Maggie, wagging her tail in proud achievement and wearing the expression that sums up her personality. The expression that says, "What?"

But despite all of her faults, we do love Maggie. And we won't ever take her back to the shelter, because number one, I don't have the heart to put her back in a cage, and number two, I'm afraid to let my wife near any kind of adoptable animals. If she had her way, we'd come home with three more dogs, plus two cats and an assortment of barnyard animals.

We would also have to consider our other dog, Casper, before stamping Maggie "Return to Sender." After all, we got Maggie as a playmate for him. So if suddenly Maggie wasn't around to bark at him, jump on him, chew his ears, hide his toys and steal his spot on the bed — well maybe it's good for Maggie that Casper doesn't have a vote.

He also doesn't have any idea how to deal with his mischievous playmate. When I come home and Maggie has played the confetti game with a week's worth of newspapers, he just looks at me like, "You know this wasn't me, right?"

Yes, I know. But I also know that given time, and possibly an exorcism, Maggie will turn into a nice dog. I think she tries to do the right thing, but sometimes forgets what the right thing is, like when she slams into the sliding glass door that she watched me close seconds before.

And when I scold her, I can tell by her sad eyes that, deep down in her soul, there's a sweet little puppy voice that just wants to say to me ...

"What?"

# The new fragrance: Eau de Snooty

If you study hard in college, graduate with honors, land a great job, make lots of money, give all the money to charity and devote your life to teaching underprivileged children with dyslexia, myopia and split ends, you too can be spit on by a perfume clerk at your local department store.

OK, they won't really spit on you. But that's just because the perfume-and-makeup contract clearly states that clerks are not allowed to spit on the customers. And the clerks never know when Ralph Lauren and the Uptight Fashion Brigade will show up on polo ponies and dish out discipline with their stylish, coordinating polo mallets ($75).

But yes, most of the clerks would love to spit on you, or at the very least, thrash you with an Armani scarf. And why not? You've got some nerve trying to buy something right in the middle of the clerk's important phone call with her boyfriend.

"NOW THAT YOU'VE RUINED THE MOMENT, WHAT DO YOU WANT?"

Looming behind the counter with heavy-duty makeup and wind-resistant hairdos, the clerks do look important. And they certainly know how important they are. After all, they know about Gucci's Magnificence, Chanel's Ambivalence and your insignificance. That's why it takes an Eternity (by Calvin Klein) for them to help any of us peons. And you better be nice or you can forget about getting a free whiff of Elizabeth Taylor's new Toilette.

I hope she cleaned it first.

I'm sure some of you don't agree with me. In that case, you probably fit into one of the following categories:

**1.** You have lots of money or act like you do by charging up your credit cards.

**2.** You have appeared in a Calvin Klein advertisement with scantily-clad 8-year-olds.

**3.** You sometimes indulge in the guilty pleasure of a rice cake and diet water.

If you fit into one of the categories, the clerks love you and you need a 12-step program. The rest of you know what I mean.

Every year I brave the potpourri-gone-mad air of the perfume, makeup and jewelry counters to buy an anniversary gift for my wife. And every year the clerks — dressed to the nines in famous-maker clothing they can't possibly afford — ignore me. They don't want to deal with a big spender dressed in a T-shirt (not-so-famous maker, $10) and shorts (I'd prefer not to reveal that, $15).

Rule No. 1: You must dress classy to get customer service.

I guess the purveyors of perfume are out of my league, at least while in clerk mode. They may be really nice people after the store closes, and they return their borrowed clothes, stop by 7-Eleven for a 12-pack of Bud and drive home in a car with a window sticker of the cartoon character Calvin peeing on the words "ex-boyfriend." But until they step out of the Gucci pumps and drop the nametag, I'm steering clear of them. I'll just go to a different department and shop for an anniversary gift.

I've always felt that nothing says "I love you" like a high-speed blender.

# Spelling is always good rule for skool

Good news high-school students of America! The latest test scores show that you are not slipping behind the rest of the world nearly as fast as predicted. In fact, many of you are performing EVEN BETTER than students in Uganda.

The bad news, however, is that some of you are just not getting it. Despite the best efforts of your teachers and MTV News, many of you don't know the basics that I learned in high school. In history, for example, I can name the exact year when George Washington led U.S. troops across the Delaware River to defeat the Nazis.

Few of you probably know that, but it's not all your fault. Our society doesn't stress the importance of education the way it stresses rock-hard abdominal muscles, money-back guarantees and Cher's new tattoo. It also seems we — and by "we" I mean everybody beyond high school age who is confused by nose rings and wide-leg jeans — may be helping you fail.

Let me explain, angry adults with cell phones.

If you design a line of educational toys, does it make sense to name your company Playskool? Sure it does, if you want children, who probably already started their day with a spelling-impaired breakfast of Froot Loops, Trix or Rice Krispies, to fail spelling tests. That spelling failure may then be a major blow to kids' self-esteem, leading them to gorge on word-mangler products like Kit Kats, Kandycorn and Kool-Aid as they kry — darn it, cry — in shame.

I'm sure you can see the spiral of doom, which I like to refer to as "The Spiral of Doom."

It's just spelling, I know, and lots of very smart people are terrible spellers. The person who invented the xylophone was one of them, as was Albert Einstein, who was so smart he couldn't spell his last name.

But spelling was the cornerstone of my education in skool — darn it, school — and it really is important. No matter how "intellugunt" you are, you won't be taken seriously unless you can spell intelligently.

So I don't envy the children who are learning how to spell cheese while eating Cheez-Whiz, Cheez-its and Cheez Doodles. For one thing, their hands are too greasy to hold a pencil. Second, it's hard for them to tell how anything is spelled, because apparently the way to market to kids is with wacky spelling. "Hey kids! You'll love Beanee Weenees! They go great with new Healthee Yummee Broccolee!"

Children's toys are also to blame. Two toys on Dr. Toy's 100 Best Toy Products list are Mr. Drumstix Music Studio and Betty Spaghetty. They are among the best toys, and yet the kids playing with them may be destined to open a business called Kustom Kar Kare and thank people for their "coroporation." Or maybe the misled children will grow up and reinvent a word like a restaurant in my neighborhood did on a banner a few months ago:

"Rally Burguer 99 cents!"

It's The Spiral of Doom, I tell you.

We must emphasize spelling. If we don't, the whole educational process will crumble. Global warming will increase, the tides will rise and certain columnists may overdramatize seemingly insignificant topics.

Most important, you high-schoolers will get lapped by the rest of the world, end up working at fast-food restaurants and be forced to ask ...

"Would you like cheez on that burguer?"

# Hey batter, I'll chatter for a cherry snow cone

It's little league baseball season again, the time when enthusiastic boys and girls step into the batter's box, choke up on the bat and dream of completing the amazing feats of their baseball heroes, like signing $10 million contract extensions.

Think of how many Pokemon cards that would buy!

But money is not what little league is all about. And even the dollar-driven, attitude-laden, Creatine-slurping world of professional baseball can't taint the beauty of the youth game. Little league is still the place where any child can learn the skills of hitting, throwing and chanting "easy out, easy out!" to crush the spirit of a 6-year-old.

Not that any of these skills are important to little leaguers, whose priorities are all out of whack. While their responsible coach is teaching them baseball basics that are invaluable to any 6-year-old, such as how to throw a brushback pitch and take out the shortstop's legs with a hard slide into second base, the little leaguers' attention is focused on who will get the cherished cherry snow cone after practice.

Come on kids, you need to get serious out there! Practice is almost over and you still don't know the infield fly rule! And Billy, would you please put the glove back on your left hand? For the last time, you're right-handed!

Most of my little league team was like Billy. We spent the game tossing our gloves in the air, adjusting our hats and praying that the ball wouldn't be hit to us. Our coach told us that we should be *hoping* that the ball would be hit to us, but he didn't have to stand out there while the giant kid (at least 4-feet tall) was about to hit a screaming line drive down our throats.

And we couldn't just concentrate on avoiding a whizzing ball that would surely end our lives. Our coach also wanted to hear some chatter, as in the "hey batter-batter" chorus that would be the perfect theme song for *A Nightmare on Sesame Street*.

Our coach couldn't get enough chatter. If the ball went through our legs, fine. If we threw it to the wrong base, fine. But God only knows the ramifications of an infield without chatter.

So the infield would rev up: "Hey batter-batter, swing batter-batter, how's it going batter-batter, if you hit it batter-batter, not at me batter-batter, I know where you live batter-batter ..."

And, oh no, he hit it!

There isn't much hitting in little league, other than kids fighting in the dugout over the spot on the bench that doesn't have splinters, so a hit is a traumatic situation. The players go into full alert, trying to remember everything they learned, like how to stay in front of the ball, watch it into the glove and throw it to first base.

Hey, which one is first base?

It can be very confusing for a little leaguer. And it's hard to think when parents are screaming "Run, run!" "Get the ball, get the ball!" and "Billy, you're RIGHT-handed!"

I always knew where first base was because I was the first baseman. When the ball was hit, I would sprint to the base and wait for the infielder to pick up the ball, look over at me, and toss the ball into left field. This happened a lot, because little leaguers throw like kiddie water sprinklers that shoot water in every direction. Anyone who has seen *America's Funniest Home Videos*, also known as *Dad Gets Hit You Know Where*, knows what I'm talking about.

There were those times, however, when the throw actually reached first base. And if the planets were aligned correctly, and our pre-pitch chatter was satisfactory, I would catch the ball while — this is hard to believe — I was also standing on the base. Then the umpire would yell "Out!" and our coach would start the kind of chatter all the players understood:

"CHERRY SNOW CONES FOR EVERYONE!"

# Cigars, bruised shins and a coach named Dad

Like the legendary hitters of professional baseball, I followed a specific routine each time I entered the batter's box. I would dig in my cleats, hike up my baggy pants, choke up on the bat, stare down the pitcher, and just as he was releasing the ball, pray that it wouldn't split my head like a melon.

I admit it wasn't quite the Joe DiMaggio theory of hitting. But to a 5-year-old, even a pitch unreachable with a telephone pole is life-threatening. I bet even the great Joltin' Joe was Boltin' Joe back when he was collecting baseball cards instead of posing for them.

At least I knew what I was supposed to do. That was thanks to my dad, who had me pegged as a future Hall of Famer from the day I was born. He even brought a baseball glove to the hospital and sat it next to me.

My dad loves baseball and wanted a son who would embrace the field of dreams. A daughter was nice, yes, and my dad knew a lot about softball. But eventually, daddy's little girl would ask for dresses instead of batting tips and talk about boys more than taking infield. At least that's how my dad had my older sister figured out.

So my dad wanted a boy. And when I was born, it was easy for him to ignore the stares of the nurses — and my mom rolling her eyes — as he strolled into the hospital with my first glove. He finally had the boy he could mold into the next Harmon Killebrew. He even had a Minnesota Twins hat waiting for me at home, which like the glove, took some growing into.

But my dad didn't care, and he soon got me hooked on baseball. When I was 3 years old, I was dragging around a plastic bat and ball. My dad would pitch to me in the front yard, and for the times when he wasn't there, he showed me how to practice by myself.

Tuck the bat under my left arm, fling the ball up with my right hand, and whammo!

My dad also took me along to his softball games, where I watched from the stands and cheered with my mom, who was usually balancing the checkbook. My mom, who got sucked into the world of little league, has never been a big sports fan. She usually brought a book or needlepoint to the games, where for two hours she would deny any connection to the guy smoking the cigar and yelling, "Come on Matt, get serious out there!"

I was 5 years old.

I actually started little league before I turned five. The league was for 5- and 6-year-olds, but my dad fudged my birthdate because he figured I could handle it. In other words, he couldn't wait.

So there I was, the absolute runt of the team, joining my teammates in that "Hey batter-batter, swing!" chant and smacking my fist into a glove that nearly swallowed up my arm. Stuck out in deep right field, you could hardly see me. But my mom did, and she was waving and rolling tape of my first game. I'm not sure if it was for posterity or so my dad could go home and evaluate my performance.

I'm just glad the video cameras of those days didn't have sound. I think it would have broken my dad's heart to hear me, in the heat of the action, telling the center fielder that I was going to get a grape snow cone after the game.

What really broke my dad's heart was years later when I tore up my arm throwing curveballs. The cliché held true in my case. Too many curveballs too early in my life meant surgery and a permanent six-inch zipper — sports lingo for a scar — on my elbow.

That was it for baseball, although my dad didn't let me go gently into retirement. How could his future superstar give up on baseball? He's a lefty, for crying out loud. He's perfect for the major leagues!

I was 12 years old.

In the blink of an eye, my dad's hopes for the second coming of Harmon Killebrew were dashed. There would be no baseball phenom to brag about to the neighbors. All those years of work and nothing to show for it.

Well, there is one thing — an incredibly grateful son. The times spent playing baseball with my dad are some of the best memories of my life. Most kids can only hope to spend as much time as I did with my dad, even if it included a bruised shin from infield practice and second-hand cigar smoke from rides to the games.

And I'll never forget that when my interest drifted toward basketball, my dad gave it his best shot. In our driveway, he showed me what he called his "George Mikan hook shot," a shot so ugly that George Mikan could've sued for defamation of character.

Well, at least my dad tried. I think that's all you can ask from a father. And I think all you can ask from a son is that he wants to be the father his dad was, and still is.

I do.

But when my son or daughter is born, I think I'll keep the basketball in the car.

# Choice cuts for a forgotten holiday

To the woman with pink hair, I'm sorry I don't remember your name. But the next time you wiggle into your purple spandex pants and drive to work for a day of split-end analysis, pondering of perms and other coif consultations, please know that you are remembered. This one's for you:

*You work a trimmer with style and grace,*
*never leaving a single hair out of place,*
*and though you wield a sharp pair of shears,*
*thanks for not cutting off one of my ears.*

Hairstylist Appreciation Day is April 30. You probably didn't know that because the hairstylist lobbying group has yet to convince Congress to make it a federal holiday. It's a tough sell for the hairstylist coalition because one of the privileges of U.S. senators and representatives, as spelled out in the U.S. Constitution, is free haircuts. But from what I've seen on C-SPAN, a free haircut doesn't always mean a good haircut. Here is my pledge to voters: My fellow Americans, like most of my colleagues I am cruising toward Baldness Boulevard, but if you elect me to work in Washington, D.C., I will never take my remaining hair, grow it long, swirl it around and create a Capitol Hill on the top of my head.

That pledge might get me elected someday, but right now I'm concentrating on the hairstylist vote. Actually, I just want to give hairstylists their due. They put up with squirming kids, complaining adults and people who ask for a haircut that will make them look like Brad Pitt. (Sir, I am a cosmetologist, not a cosmetic surgeon).

They also have some of the most annoying, irresponsible,

inconsiderate and worst-dressed co-workers on the planet. I don't actually know who the co-workers are, but they are the topic of conversation each time I get a trim.

"Do you know that she was late again for work yesterday?" one barber/stylist/hair-quality technician will say to the other. "And once again, she didn't clean up her station."

Sometimes it makes them so mad that they just want to scream, or in my case, pull on my hair harder as they cut it. Yes, I feel their pain.

Despite everything they go through, hairstylists don't even get their own week. In fact, they don't even get their own day. Hairstylists share April 30 with National Honesty Day, a strange combination considering most men, at least the smart ones, are never honest with their wives when asked, "Do you like my new haircut?"

So here is my tribute to hairstylists, who teach us all about haircare, and also that "babely" and "hunky" are actual words. (We've all been forced to read one of those teen magazines while we wait, right?):

*I walk into the waiting room,*
*put my name onto the list,*
*"How long is the wait?" I ask,*
*"Just 10 minutes," you insist.*

*In a flash I'm in the chopping chair,*
*I barely even had to sit,*
*"How do you want your hair done?"*
*"Make me look like Brad Pitt."*

*You get right to work,*
*a trim here, a clip there,*
*and I know in just minutes,*
*I'll be out of that chair.*

*So remember you're appreciated,*
*that's what this column is about,*
*and I'll always sing your praises,*
*or at least 'til my hair falls out.*

Next week: Another unrecognized holiday earns poetic justice, assuming I can find something that rhymes with Hairball Awareness.

# The hairy truth about balding relationships

Men get a lot of relationship advice. They are told to listen better, show compassion, be more appreciative, be more understanding, take charge, back down, step out of their "emotional caves" and step on spiders in the garage. With all that advice, it's no surprise men occasionally get so busy working on their relationships that they forget to help with the housework for a day or two, or maybe a week, or perhaps during the Clinton Administration.

Fortunately, all the advice can be simplified. Experts have identified four strategies to help men maintain lasting relationships with their significant others. They are: Respecting your partner, developing good communication, learning to compromise and never going bald.

The first three strategies come from noted relationship expert John Gray, the author of *Men are from Mars, Women are from Venus*. The final strategy comes from noted hair-regrowth expert Rogaine, which is currently airing a commercial to prove its point.

The scene: A man — ironically the same man who in an earlier commercial sought a doctor's advice for heartburn — steps up to the camera, and with his wife or girlfriend in the background, asks, "Will she still feel the same way if I lose my hair?"

His answer: "Sure ... She'll just feel it about someone else."

Well, I certainly feel silly after seeing that Rogaine commercial. For years I've concentrated on avoiding a fallout with my wife when I should have focused on my own fallout. The fallout that began shortly after college and has reached the point where I'm actually happy to find new gray hairs, because at least they haven't abandoned ship.

After watching the commercial, and a few more of my hairs

drift to the ground, I decided to ask Rogaine about its shallow view of society. Here's the response I got from Rogaine's consumer affairs department:

"We try hard to create positive, interesting and informative advertising that appeals to our target audience."

Striking fear into men is "positive"? Were other ads rejected because they weren't positive enough? Was a commercial proposed featuring a woman berating a man about his bald spot until he curls into a fetal position and weeps in a closet?

OK, so it's just a commercial. And anything from the world where people dive out of airplanes for diet sodas and openly discuss adult undergarments probably isn't indicative of reality. But it's easy to get sucked into the "Hairanoia" propagated by Rogaine and other hair regenerators and rejuvenators.

"It's all about confidence!" says one anti-balding Web site, which features a man with a dynamite head of hair basking in the glow of a horde of women attracted to his masculine mane. "A full head of hair helps a man's self-esteem."

Maybe so, but appearance probably isn't the best basis for your self-esteem. I learned that long ago. It wasn't the day my parents told me that everyone is unique or the many days that my teachers uttered the "You are special!" mantra in grammar school. It was the day I discovered that, from every angle, and in even the most flattering light, I could never pass for a Ralph Lauren model.

Most men can't, but thankfully most women aren't like the superficial significant other in the Rogaine commercial. A friend of mine backed me up on this, saying she found the commercial offensive. But ...

"I do think some women would be shallow enough to leave a guy who is losing his hair," she said. "But at what point does a woman say, 'OK, You've lost too much hair now. I'm leaving.' How many times does she have to find his hair in the drain? Does she keep a list? It doesn't just happen overnight, you know."

No, it takes years. Just like it takes years to develop a relationship that is deeper than a pretty face, rock-hard abdominals and healthy, manageable hair. Just like it takes years to appreciate that, while bald might not be beautiful, it sure beats a relationship that can't survive getting a little thin on top.

# Help needed on the loofah aisle

After an exhaustive five-person study, I've discovered that many people suffer "time gaps" when driving. An explanation of time gaps: A driver arrives at a destination and can't remember large portions of the trip, like getting on the freeway, stopping at a toll booth or accidentally running a Girl Scout off the road.

This is sometimes called "subconscious driving." Others refer to it as "hypnotic driving" or the time their Girl Scout cookies were delivered by a member of the Personal Injury Trial Lawyers Association.

Whatever the term, time gaps also apply to driving a shopping cart. I learned this last week during an exhausting one-person research study, also known as the search for Oil Free Deep Action Cream Cleanser.

Oil Free Deep Action Cream Cleanser was on my wife's shopping list, and I decided to do the shopping this week. I should have known where the cream cleanser was because I'm often at the grocery store when she buys it, but apparently she picks it out while I am suffering time gaps at the helm of the cart. Either that or I am focusing on the Muzak flowing from the loudspeakers. I never knew there was an orchestral version of AC/DC's "Back in Black."

On my own this time, I looked at the list and began the analysis. Oil Free Deep Action Cream Cleanser: Is it a body wash, a face wash or a member of the family of exfoliates, wrinkle-relaxers and rejuvenators? Is it by the bars of soap or the rows of perfumes and make-up?

My final analysis was that I needed help.

"I think it's by the loofah sponges," one woman told me as I, my shopping cart, and a small rock wedged in one of the wheels of the cart rumbled past her and the bars of soap.

Her suggestion could've helped because, at the risk of tumbling from a mountain of masculinity, I know what a loofah sponge is. But I didn't know where the loofah sponges were in the store. That was probably one of the SAT questions I got wrong: A loofah sponge is to a bar of Irish Spring as Oil Free Deep Action Cream Cleanser is to ...

I have no idea. That's why I didn't get into Yale.

Frustrated by the search, and with a bottle of Mrs. Dash seasoning looming on the list, I decided to build my confidence. I picked out the apples, bananas, cereal, cheese and hamburger buns. Then I stepped up to the challenge of finding tomato sauce and tomato paste among the sliced tomatoes, diced tomatoes, tomato puree and Italian paste. No problem.

But eventually I had to return to the search for Oil Free Deep Action Cream Cleanser. It wasn't by the Oil of Olay, the hair coloring or the Lady Speed Stick. It wasn't by the press-on nails, tanning lotions or age-defying teeth-whiteners. It wasn't by the row of extra-strength pimple-fighters, where several leaders of tomorrow were searching for a solution to their clogged pores of today.

This was way too complicated. I remember when I was single, and I could find everything I needed. My only worry then was remembering to tell the cashier that the antifungal cream was for athlete's foot and not its other use, masculine itch.

In the middle of my nostalgic daydream, I stumbled upon the loofah sponges. And next to the loofah sponges was the Oil Free Deep Action Cleaning Cleanser, available in a tube or pump. I got one of each, figuring my wife would be happy with one or the other.

I also bought her some flowers. Why not? My successful search left me brimming with confidence, and flowers would get me extra mileage out of the shopping favor.

More important, I thought I should arrive home as Mr. Romantic because I was arriving without the Mrs. Dash.

# Sometimes, 'I love you' is too easy

Those three little words can be so hard to say. You're nervous, confused and vulnerable all at once. And when you tell someone "I love you" for the first time, you have no idea what the response will be.

Especially if you accidentally say those three little words to the person cashing your check at the bank. Or to the person bagging your groceries. Or to a telemarketer offering you a great deal on vinyl siding.

Can this really happen?

Well, I think it's just a matter of time before it happens to me. The other day I was talking on the phone with one of my *Dallas Morning News* co-workers, discussing important newspaper topics like what stories should be written, how to improve headlines and the best ways to get newsprint off our hands. And when the conversation ended, I nearly said "I love you."

Now that's frightening. We have a friendly atmosphere at work, but that would be crossing the line. I'm sure it would be included in my annual evaluation under interpersonal skills:

"Once said 'I love you' to the person who fixed the copier."

Thankfully, that's still a fictional account of my embarrassment. But I'm teetering on nonfiction because "I love you" always feels like the right thing to say at the end of a coversation. It's the "talk to you later" substitute that, when used at the office, would have lots of people talking later.

This is a marriage byproduct I never expected. A lot of Home and Garden Television, yes, I knew that was coming. Weekly arrivals of magazines with Oprah on the cover, yes, of course. A smattering of requests to kill the big spider in the corner of the kitchen, certainly. I almost expected that to be in the wedding vows.

But saying "I love you" the first time was so difficult, why does it come so easily — too easily — now?

Well, every day my wife and I talk on the phone, and we end the conversation with "I love you." That's not evidence of some incredibly romantic relationship, it's just something we started doing when we got married.

But when you say it that much, you burn a trail. And that trail is so well-marked, I'm afraid I'll say "I love you" to the pizza delivery guy. Either that or I'll ask him if we can please watch something other than Home and Garden Television.

Worse than saying "I love you" to a co-worker is the thought that these words have lost some value. The words once meant so much that my throat locked up trying to say them. Now I nearly say them to the sandwich artist who puts the right amount of mustard on my turkey hero.

There shouldn't be anything more powerful than "I love you." Nothing should be more endearing or more welcomed by the person with whom you chose to share your life and the remote. So somehow I need to bring the meaning back to the words.

If absence really makes the heart grow fonder, the answer might be to say "I love you" less. But I don't think that will go over well. If my wife says "I love you," and I respond with "Right back at ya," it won't be long before the author of *Men are from Mars, Women are from Venus* is in my living room asking me why I've decided to lock up my feelings in my Martian cave.

I think I just need to remember why I first said the words. I need to remember the reasons I have for loving my wife, the reasons she makes me happy, the reasons why I should never compromise the value of "I love you" by using it for reckless purposes like ending a column.

But it just comes so easily. I love you.

# Here comes the bride ... She wants a breadmaker

Some people hate gift registries. To them, gift lists are impersonal, cramp creativity, and even more tragic, never include handmade purple ceramic lamps shaped like elephants. Or limited-edition Chia Pets. Or the hilarious singing fish they are certain is the perfect gift.

This is why I strongly support gift registries.

Those of you who have unwrapped a hand-carved wooden flamingo on your special day know what I mean. And you also know that, had you registered for gifts, I would've sent you something better.

I also would've saved a lot of time. Gift lists are great for that. But most important, gift lists make it impossible to buy the wrong gift.

At least that's what I thought before I helped pick out a wedding gift last week.

"You can't get them a set of bowls and ONE placemat," my wife said. "They registered for eight placemats."

"I know they registered for eight," I said, squinting at the wedding-gift wish list. "Somebody else can get them the other seven. The set of bowls and one placemat add up to fifty dollars."

Fifty dollars was our budget for the wedding gift, which doesn't go far in a world of $150 table linens and $500 cookware sets. But we were limited to an amount collected from co-workers of the bride-to-be, who is a teacher. And before anyone calls teachers chintzy, you should know how often they get hit up at work for gifts. Five bucks for Julie's wedding gift. Five bucks for Mary's baby gift. Five bucks for Bob, the teacher who is collecting because his nephew's neighbor, Timmy, has a best friend who turns six this month.

So we were strapped financially. But my wife was determined to find the right wedding gift. And as a good husband, I was determined to help her as long as it took no more than 15 minutes.

"OK. So we'll get them all eight placemats," I said. "And then we can get them the two pillows they want."

That wouldn't cut it. "The placemats are for the kitchen and the pillows are for the bedroom," my wife said. "They don't really go together."

Why does that matter? They're both wedding gifts. Couldn't we just wrap the placemats and pillows in one box and call it the breakfast-in-bed collection?

We moved on to the tableware area, where the happy couple had registered for some plates. Add in tax, a card and some wrapping paper, and the cost would be right at fifty bucks. The search was over.

"But the plates are blue," my wife said. "I don't like them."

"But the bride and groom like them. They put them on their list," I said. "Isn't that what's important?"

Not important enough to end the search. So we walked over to housewares. We looked at griddles, pressure-cookers, breadmakers and bake sets. We crunched the numbers and tried to find the gift or gifts that best said, "Good luck on your marriage, we only had 50 bucks."

But nothing fit the criteria. So I decided to initiate the speed round of our shopping game, throwing out anything that added up to the right amount. "A coffeemaker and a wall clock ... two vinyl chairs and an accent rug ... the George Foreman Lean, Mean Grilling Machine and a bath towel ..."

"A grilling machine and a bath towel?" my wife asked.

Well, I said, if you're standing over a grill for even a few minutes, you'll be sweaty enough to need a shower. Then you'll have a new bath towel to use. I thought it was perfect.

Still, we decided on a different gift. I can't say what it was because the gift recipients might read this, but I can say that even gift registries won't save you from the ugly truth of gift-giving.

It's never just the thought that counts.

# Sweetest Day is bitter pill for men

As a member of the global community of husbands and boyfriends, also known as Men Who Fear Feminine Retribution For Missing The Anniversary Of Some Special Day Like The First Time We Went Grocery Shopping Together, I would like to reprimand the person responsible for the latest way to make us feel like unromantic clods.

Sweetest Day. Who came up with that holiday?

"A woman," I can hear all the men saying.

Now isn't that a typical unfeeling response from the male population? Men should be ashamed for callously tossing the blame on the other gender, which is already suffering this week because we haven't noticed their new haircuts. (Men, it's a good policy to compliment your mate's hair every day. Say it makes them look young and thin.)

The truth is, a *man* started Sweetest Day. But before you demand his name so you can thrash him with the dozen roses you just spent quality beer money on, you should know this:

He's dead.

More important, he had good intentions. About 70 years ago, a candy manufacturer in Cleveland rounded up his friends and neighbors to distribute candy at an orphanage. It was a day to remember the town's forgotten and spread joy to those less fortunate. But his wife, named Sweetest, was angry that her husband was gone all day. She wouldn't let him back in the house until he named the day after her and bought her a dozen long-stemmed roses, a box of chocolates and a card with romantic verses in iambic pentameter.

At least the orphanage part of that is true. And that's why we now celebrate Sweetest Day every third Saturday in October.

Well, some of us do. I wasn't aware of the holiday until this year, when the coalition of florists, candy-makers and greeting card companies — also known as The Coalition Determined To Get More Money From Unromantic Clods — started the hard sell on Sweetest Day.

Apparently the coalition finally noticed the appalling lack of holidays in October. And think about it ... Other than Halloween, there's only Yom Kippur, National Children's Day, Canadian Thanksgiving, Columbus Day, Bosses Day, Alaska Day, Farmer's Day, Mother-In-Law's Day and United Nations Day. That's simply not enough Hallmark moments.

So the coalition met, and Sweetest Day got the nod, nudging out Dental Hygiene Awareness Day, Bald-Headed Appreciation Day and Step-Nephew-In-Law Day. The florists and candy-makers were strongly in favor of also adding Colonic Health Day, which seemed like a good choice because it served a noble purpose and affected everyone. But the card companies vetoed the idea because they couldn't find any words that rhymed with polyp or colonoscopy.

That's fine, because we already have enough holidays to forget. And speaking again for the global community of husbands and boyfriends, also known as the Group of Significant Others Who Are Supposed To Kill All the Spiders and Be Very Brave When Things Go Bump in the Night, our minds can't handle it all. With anniversaries, birthdays, Valentine's Day and remembering to put the toilet seat down, our minds are cluttered. A few more holidays and we're liable to snap. You'll find us wandering the streets, telling strangers that we like their new haircuts.

For now, I offer this to all the other husbands and boyfriends. When Sweetest Day comes around next year, you don't need to spend money on a card. Here is a poem guaranteed to please:

*Sweetest I love you beyond compare,*
*so I always wear a grin,*
*and remember that I like your hair,*
*it makes you look young and thin.*

# It's Vegas! Bring the kids (and an oxygen mask)

Here's a piece of Las Vegas information to impress your friends (well, if they are easily impressed): Translated into English, Las Vegas means "the meadows."

Now isn't that a fitting name? Just like a beautiful meadow, Las Vegas thrives on understated, humble charm — as in a 50-foot billboard photo of Wayne Newton.

"Welcome Back, Mr. Las Vegas!" it says.

For everyone else, welcome to another world. A world featuring high rollers, low morals and entertainers from the Elvis Era who can still pack auditoriums with the routines they performed 20 years ago on the Jerry Lewis Telethon. A world that will take your breath away, either with its magnificent, glowing hotels or its glitzy, glamorous secondhand smoke.

Las Vegas definitely is the smoker's vacation. With cigarette vending machines in every casino, it's a throwback to the golden age of lighting up. A time when the Marlboro Man and Joe Camel weren't as hated as a person wearing fur; a time when restaurants and airplane flights allowed people to smoke; a time when the world was less concerned with trivial matters like lung cancer.

For the most part, however, Las Vegas strives to be modern. New eye-popping hotels line The Strip, each attempting to out-Vegas the other. (I know Vegas isn't a verb, but no other verb applies to a place that has an Egyptian pyramid, medieval castle and the Statue of Liberty on the same street.)

There's also a volcano, a circus, and the Eiffel Tower on The Strip. They're part of each hotel's theme, which is reflected in architecture, guest rooms and shopping areas. The Venetian, for example, is a tribute to Venice. So it has Italian shops, a canal with gondola rides and a lesser-known aspect of Italian culture: the 24-hour steak-and-eggs buffet for just $7.99.

The Venetian might be stretching Italian culture, but every Vegas hotel has a buffet. Every hotel *must* have a buffet to attract the Las Vegas crowd, much of which is on the downward slope of the bell curve and has traveled on cruise ships, where it's all food, all the time. Buffets rule in Vegas, where vacationers will stand in Disneyland-like lines for "all you care to eat." It used to be called "all you can eat," but apparently some people took that as a personal challenge.

The real personal challenge is sticking to moderation once you leave the theme world for the casino world. That's because no matter what they look like on the outside, the casinos are all the same on the inside. Flashing lights, music and decoration tempt you to drink up, have fun and spend last week's paycheck. And if you're on a bit of a losing streak, the card dealers and slot machines accept all major credit cards. They'll probably accept your firstborn to keep you in the casino.

And why not bring your firstborn and the rest of the kids? Las Vegas is billing itself as a family destination, and the trip can be very educational.

For one thing, every hotel is a lesson in engineering. The nightly topless dance revue is also a good teaching tool for biology. And the dinner buffet is the perfect opportunity to talk about world hunger — "Son, how would you feel if you couldn't get that third piece of cake?"

Casinos are also the perfect place to teach math skills and money management: Why hasn't daddy won any money? Because the odds are so against him. Why can't the family go to Sea World as planned? Because daddy keeps playing.

Sadly, kids miss out on the final part of that education because they aren't allowed in casinos. But someday Las Vegas will change that rule so the whole family can enjoy the smokiest meadow on the planet.

Until then, maybe kids could pass the time by taking rides on Joe Camel. He's still looking for work.

# With this ring, I thee appreciate

Five years hardly make me a wily veteran at the marriage game, but I have learned a lot since my unforgettable wedding day in June of 1996.

Or was it July?

Just kidding, of course. I'll never be the uncaring, insensitive sort who forgets his anniversary. I couldn't forget a day that was the start of something beautiful, a day that changed my life, a day that my wife had tattooed on my forearm when the ceremony ended.

Seriously, I have enjoyed my four years of marriage. But it has been a big learning experience. I've learned more about Lifetime television, figure skating and the importance of matching a bedspread with curtains than I ever expected. I've also learned that certain people cannot sleep unless they are on the same side of the bed every night, and that certain people think everything they wear makes them look fat.

As you can see, I've also learned to speak in vague terms so that certain people can't incriminate me with this column.

But the most important thing I've learned over the past four years, with the help of those same "certain people," is the real definition of love. Here it is:

Love is being able to use the $1.50 off coupon at Olive Garden.

That's right, it's the true-love discount. When I go out with my wife, I boldly put my coupons on the table. Free drink, free appetizer, buy one get one free entrees, and "Excuse me, waiter, but I think you forgot to knock the 50 cents off my hot wings."

A guy can't do that when he's dating. He must impress the woman, which means not revealing certain details, like how his salary as Slurpee-machine cleaner won't cover the Surf and Turf. He'll tell his date to order whatever she wants, and then pray she doesn't get the lobster. And what if she wants to start with an appetizer, have a little wine *and* some dessert? He'll either have to settle for having the side salad as his dinner or risk hitting his Visa limit. And as all guys know, it better be one incredible date if you're going to be making payments on it for six months.

I've never had to make payments on a date, but then again, I didn't date much before I got married. I guess it was because I was very selective — I only dated women who said "Yes" when I asked them out.

I'm sure glad that's all over. For me, asking a woman out was harder than asking for one of her kidneys. My approach was so smooth, some of them probably would've offered me a kidney in lieu of a date.

It was also a rare occasion when I had a good opening line. And even if I came up with something clever, my mind would go blank at the big moment and my pick-up line would become something like, "Is that mustard on your shirt?"

As I said, I didn't date much.

And for that I'm very thankful. I never had to lie in a personal ad, never had to go on a blind date and never fell in love with a woman on the Internet and discovered later that she was actually a truck driver named Ed.

Yes, I got lucky. And five years after starting my prison sentence, I still love everything about it.

I know "certain people" like to hear that.

# Welcome to dog ownership: Now sit

Many of you added the joy of floppy ears and drool to your house recently. Congratulations! Studies have proven that dogs help their human companions live longer, happier lives — unless they trip them while chasing a tennis ball down the stairs at 2 a.m.

But happiness and longevity aside, your dog keeps getting in the trash. And he jumps on the bed. And he wants to "help" you read the newspaper. What can you do?

I'm glad you asked, because I'm the owner of two extremely well-behaved dogs. It wasn't always that way, of course, but with patience, discipline and advanced training techniques, the dogs now obey my every command when I have food in my hands.

Without bribery at my fingertips, things are a bit more difficult. But considering my dogs have yet to attack a 3-year-old, at least successfully, and have not chewed up a roll of wrapping paper in the past 24 hours, I consider myself an authority on animal control.

Control is the key. You must let your dog know who is boss and make sure it knows the rules. For example, one rule at my house is that dogs are not allowed on the furniture. This rule was created when we adopted Maggie, a Corgi mix that sheds enough hair each day to keep a family of four warm during a Milwaukee winter.

Unfortunately, both dogs misunderstood this rule as "Dogs are not allowed on the couch unless humans are not home." Later when I ran out of food to bribe them with, the rule was amended to "Dogs are allowed on the couch, but humans can also sit there."

This may seem like the rule was a failure, but it was actually a good thing. It opened a line of communication between me and my dogs, or as we call it in the dog-training business — "family negotiation." It's just like when the 16-year-old son asks for a later curfew in exchange for not drinking, crashing the car into anything or getting someone pregnant.

Family negotiation has become very popular with my dogs, especially Casper, a West Highland Terrier with the smarts of Lassie and the contractual savvy of a sports agent. His incessant barking helped form the following contract: Dogs agree not to pee on the carpet as long as humans open the back door anytime dogs need to pee, chase a plastic bag or make threatening growling sounds at the 3-year-old next door.

The dogs have also agreed to no longer engage in activities like swallowing small plastic objects and licking pesticide, which would require more emergency trips to the veterinarian in the middle of the night. In exchange, the dogs received rights to tipping over wastebaskets, shredding newspapers and a chew toy to be named later.

This kind of flexibility is important to a happy owner-dog relationship. You don't want the dog on the bed? Then be flexible and give it a dog bed of its own. And when the dog decides to ignore its own bed and jump on your bed, you'll need to be flexible enough to find a comfortable position for sleeping.

The important thing is to maintain control. Sure, I've given in to many of the dogs' demands, but I've always received compensation. There are now nightly treats before bed, but in exchange, Casper agreed to sleep on only half of my pillow. And there was the demand for longer walks and two trips to the park each week, but that allows me peace of mind knowing that Maggie won't drag certain articles of laundry into the living room when we have friends over.

I can even write this entire column without either dog jumping on the keyboard. In exchange, all I had to do was fdskfslfFDGFKPSDKG.

I guess the dogs decided it's time to renegotiate.

# Tube socks are cleared for takeoff

This week I got some good news in my fight against the aging process: A guy at the airport called me "dude" instead of "sir." It was refreshing to learn that I still qualify as a dude to at least one person, even if that person had green hair.

Of course with the good comes the bad, and this week featured another milestone on my road to becoming either a well-adjusted adult or a bitter bald man who mumbles about stock fluctuation and wears tube socks with dress pants. (I'm hoping to take the right path when the road forks in a few years.)

So what happened this week?

It wasn't a typical warning sign of getting older, like emerging gray hairs, a forehead that needs a lot more sunblock to cover it or a sudden interest in the fiber content of Cocoa Puffs. It was my latest airplane flight, which I hated.

The scary part is the airline did just about everything right. The flight attendant mentioned that we would be flying from Dallas to Dallas, which didn't inspire a lot of confidence in the crew, and another flight attendant rolled over a man's foot with the beverage cart, but that was it.

Still, from the moment we took off to the moment we landed, I wanted to get off the plane.

Maybe it was the person who sat next to me and found it incredibly fascinating that we both had red hair. I mean, what are the odds?

Maybe it was the interesting article I read in the airline's magazine about the world-renowned chefs that were overseeing each flight's meal. I could certainly taste their input in the breakfast of Cheerios and a banana.

Or maybe I'm just getting older.

Whatever the reason, this wasn't the airborne amusement park I remembered as a kid, when the best part of the family vacation was getting to fly on the plane. Back then it was exciting to take off, land and watch the world pass by from the window seat. On the plane, the Coke tasted better, the peanuts were an amazing treat, and it was great to be able to push the call button for the flight attendant anytime I wanted.

OK, it's not right to keep pushing the call button. But it was funny to see how mad the flight attendants would get. And at 9 years old, you can get away with just about anything. At 29, however, an itchy trigger finger on the call button will earn your luggage "priority handling," if you know what I mean.

Eating in the airport was also exciting when I was a kid, although it was pretty much the same food everywhere, with a different name depending on the location. In Minnesota, it was the Midwestern Cafe, in Arizona it was the Desert Cafe and in California it was the Beach Cafe. To me, each cafe was "fancy shmancy," a phrase my brother coined at age 5 when we walked into Pancho's Mexican Buffet. For those of you who don't know, Pancho's is the ultra-chic restaurant where you raise the flag on your table when you want some more chow.

I no longer find the airport cafes fancy shmancy, although they still fill me with wonder. I now wonder how a bagel and orange juice can cost seven bucks.

These are the wonders of being an adult. Instead of wondering how many Cokes I can get in a two-hour flight, and whether I will get the mug with my name on it or the hat that says "San Diego" from the gift shop, I'm wondering if my flight will be late.

And what happens if I miss my connecting flight? What if my rental-car reservation has been lost? What if I end up in Denver while my luggage is doing laps at the baggage claim in Des Moines?

What will I do without my tube socks and dress pants?

# Whine on Americans, it's your right

Soon Americans of all ages will flock to the nearest open space to celebrate the independence of their country. They'll sit in lawn chairs and on blankets, watch the fireworks explode in beautiful colors, and ooh and ah over the patriotic feeling they get when Calamine lotion is rubbed on their mosquito bites.

That's what America is all about. Sitting in a park, watching people dance around with glow-in-the dark tubes on their head and listening to them remix "The Star Spangled Banner":

*"The bombs and their glare,*
*the rockets burstin' in the air,*
*gave proof 'til one night,*
*that our fight wasn't fair..."*

My strategy for patriotic songs is to lip sync the parts I don't know. As for "America the Beautiful," I don't even try the second verse because all I can remember is that it has a line about pilgrims' feet.

Still, the fireworks show and sing-a-long is a lot of fun for everybody. But when all the explosions, singing and mosquito-slapping is over, the complaints begin. The show was too short, the fireworks weren't that great, and just look at the traffic. I mean, can't the government do something about that?

My dad did something about it. We would leave the show early to miss the traffic, as well as the end of the fireworks.

"You already saw a blue one, a green one and a red one," he would say as his kids followed him out of the park while glancing back at the big finale. "You'll see more fireworks next year."

At least we could go home and watch more fireworks in our neighborhood. Somebody was always shooting off illegal fireworks in a backyard. These were the people who decided to take patriotic celebrations into their own hands, and risk losing one of those hands by lighting fireworks they bought from a booth on the side of the road.

Every year a letter to the editor would appear in the newspaper a week before Independence Day, warning people of the dangers of fireworks and asking, "How can the government let people get these fireworks? Why doesn't the government do something about this?"

Now that's what America is *really* about. If there's anything that brings America's melting pot to a unified boil, it's our freedom to whine about our government. People of all ages, races, religions — even those who spent $19.95 to proudly display the Louie the Largemouth Bass singing fish in their homes — have the right to complain.

This right began with the Declaration of Independence back in 1776, which was written by Thomas Jefferson. The Declaration of Independence was approved by the Continental Congress on — this is more than a coincidence — July 4. I'm sure many of you knew that, but you'd be surprised how many people don't know the significance of July 4. And even more shocking, many of these people do not proudly display Louie the Largemouth Bass in their homes.

Anyway, the Declaration of Independence stated that all men are created equal, that they are endowed by their Creator with certain unalienable rights, and that among those rights are life, liberty and the pursuit of happiness. Over the years, it has been expanded to include the right to no payments for 90 days, the right to an attorney who will fight for you and the right to be rewarded for your good credit.

More than two centuries after its inception, that astounding, historic, whining document still rings true. That's why, although the United States has some flaws, we should be thankful to live in a country that gives us the freedom to whine about it. And that's why when the show ends this Independence Day, you won't see me complaining about the quality of the fireworks or the lack of parking spaces. You won't even see me complaining about the patriotic parade of traffic heading for the highways.

In fact, you won't see me at all. I'll be exercising my freedom to leave before the finale.

# I'm a poet, but the cards won't know it

*Starting a column is never easy,*
*sometimes it even makes me queasy,*
*but today just to keep you reading,*
*I'll begin with a stupid four-line greeting.*

A couple of years ago I wrote a column about how I could never find a good greeting card. It came right after I struggled to find the right card for a friend, who ended up with a crazy duck hoping his birthday would be a quack up.

Well, apparently it's true that the squeaky wheel gets the grease, or in my case, an offer to write greeting cards. Yep, this week an online pundit of special-day poetry offered me the chance to write some of its cards. So I sent them this idea, which I believe fills a market niche that is often neglected:

*Hope your birthday is Da Bomb,*
*cooler than anything dot.com,*
*so make this day like no other,*
*and keep it real, word to your mother.*

Funky, hip-hoppin' youngsters want to send birthday greetings too, right? And they can't possibly face their friends after sending a card that says, "I hope on your special day, tidings of joy will come your way."

They might as well include a Yanni CD.

Of course, there are many other market voids that I believe greeting cards could address. For example, I never see cards for a person who has lost a job:

*I'm sorry to hear you lost your job,*
*that you need to start saving pennies,*
*but remember if you fake your age,*
*you can still get a deal at Denny's.*

See, that's not only uplifting, it has a helpful tip about stretching your dollar. And I think that's the key to improving greeting cards — incorporating the Barbara-Streisand-movie emotion with useful information. Putting that idea into practice, here is a birthday card for a teenager:

*Happy birthday to a fine young man,*
*who always does the best he can,*
*and if he wants to be super cool,*
*he'll keep off drugs and stay in school.*

Furthering that idea, here is a get-well card for an ailment rarely addressed:

*I know you're feeling down in the dumps,*
*because your rash has itchy bumps,*
*but remember as you start to scratch,*
*that will just make it worse, you idiot.*

OK, I admit that last line needs some work. But I think you get the idea.

The card company, however, did not. In fact, it wasn't too thrilled about any of my submissions, probably because my cards are too specific to attract enough buyers. That and not many people will admit to an itchy rash.

It all comes down to making money, which is why I suggested to the card company that it use corporate tie-ins for its cards. That way it can make the cards more specific and more meaningful while preserving the bottom line. Here's one I'm going to send in:

*Heard you're trying to lose some weight,*
*that soon you'll reduce what's on your plate,*
*well if that diet just isn't your thing,*
*Whoppers are on sale at Burger King.*

If they don't like that one either, I'm not giving up. I've already started a new one that combines a birthday greeting with a strong anti-smoking message and an advertisement for a nicotine patch. And I've got an idea for a 35th birthday card that promotes Kellogg's All-Bran and an important health note.

Does anyone know a word that rhymes with colonoscopy?

# Studies can be hazardous to your health

A health study came out recently with results that were, as is always the case, disturbing. If you didn't see it with a big headline in the newspaper or on the television news right before the story about the new baby zebra at the zoo, here it is:

A University of Southern California study found that taking vitamin C pills may speed up hardening of the arteries. The study found that those taking the pills had "accelerated thickening of the walls of the big arteries in their necks," and furthermore, that USC rules and will kick UCLA's butt in every sport next season.

Well, everything except that last part. But the most shocking element of the story was the reason it gave that people take vitamin C. In theory, the story said, vitamin C and some other nutrients might protect the circulatory system and other organs by suppressing the damaging effects of oxygen.

The DAMAGING effects of oxygen! The one thing that I always felt safe indulging in is apparently damaging my body. I guess the road to good health includes avoiding vitamin C pills and holding your breath for long periods of time. Maybe we should all start smoking. Doesn't that take oxygen out of the blood?

OK, we shouldn't all start smoking. After all, the overwhelming medical evidence, surgeon general's warnings and after-school specials have convinced me that smoking is not a good decision, unless you want to look cool in high school or star in a blockbuster movie. And as an addicted 30-year-old, it's hard to look cool with a dozen nicotine patches stuck to your arm while you chew nicotine gum and try to bum a cigarette off a teenager.

But other than the health studies on smoking, few reports are very clear. Especially with reports on nutrition, where every revelation eventually gets contradicted and no expert agrees on anything. Pasta is good for you, but wait, you may be a carbohydrate addict. Don't eat foods high in cholesterol, but wait, is that good cholesterol or bad cholesterol?

And then there are eggs, which do the good-bad flip-flop more often than a character in a soap opera. Eggs have lots of cholesterol, fear them! Eggs have lots of protein, eat them! Now the local yolk-els of the egg community assure us that eggs can be a great part of a heart-healthy diet. But I figure even a Twinkies-and-Pop Tarts splurge can be part of a heart-healthy diet if you eat celery sticks and sprouts the rest of the week.

Now that sounds like quite a diet. Maybe I'll write a book on it.

Until then, there are many other diets to choose from. Each is proven to work by actual photographs of men and women who, BEFORE, looked overweight and very unhappy, and AFTER, look very pleased to be sucking in their stomachs and stretching out their necks to look thinner. The before photos are usually in black-and-white and shot in trailer parks, whereas the after photos are in color and are shot in upscale areas.

The real estate-diet connection. Another book idea.

Of course, my brilliant ideas will soon be contradicted by experts. And considering that I'm about to slather on sunblock for another day of pale face vs. the ultraviolet rays, my diet ideas will probably be debunked right under the headline that says "Sunblock shown to cause cancer in laboratory rats."

It just seems that good advice never holds up. So what can we do?

I think I'm going to hold my breath and hope for the best. And maybe have another Twinkie.

# Pull out your wallet or I'll clean you out

You probably didn't hear about it, but last week my wife and I were held hostage in our home. Nobody was hurt, and although there were a few tense moments, it ended in the best way possible — by giving me a column idea.

It was a typical Tuesday evening. My wife was working on her lesson plans for school, I was forgetting to put the dishes in the dishwasher, and our dogs were bravely defending the house from a squirrel, a plastic bag blowing in the wind and their archenemy, the 3-year-old from next door. Our dogs hate the 3-year-old because his mom used to control him with a leash that attached to his wrist, but unlike our dogs, he now gets to roam freely because he doesn't chase garbage trucks.

It was about 8 p.m. when we heard the knock on the door. I opened the door, and a desperate woman asked if she could come in. "You would really be helping me out," she said.

So we let her in, and I immediately knew it was a mistake. She walked into the living room, dropped a big box on the floor and pulled out the heavy artillery — the new Kirby vacuum-shampooer-cleaning machine. It was a machine that would change our lives, and get this, she was willing to show us how for free!

"How could we have let this person in?" I thought. Then I remembered, we're morons. A few months ago we raced to the post office to find out, by certified mail, about a major prize we had won. It turns out that our major prize was the opportunity to see an exciting presentation on how to pay lots of money to become a member of a country club. I would have preferred one of the other major prizes, like the five-function LCD watch.

Anyway, our vacuum vendor started the demonstration-to-end-all-demonstrations. She didn't just sprinkle some sugar on the floor and vacuum it up. She vacuumed the carpet, the walls, our bed and even offered an attachment that could be used to vacuum the dogs.

Needless to say, our dogs have a new archenemy.

Each time she vacuumed something, she would show us how much dirt was picked up. "Did you know you were living in all this dirt?" she asked.

I didn't have an answer.

And she didn't have an answer when I asked how much the vacuum cost. In fact, over an hour had passed and we still didn't know the price. She just kept vacuuming things, and I started to hope her cleaning service was the major prize I've been promised so many times and never received.

But of course it wasn't. As she was starting to shampoo the living-room carpet, she handed me the price.

$2,100.

"That's a lot of money for a vacuum," I said.

"And a shampooer," she said.

I laughed at the prospect of owning a vacuum worth more than my first car.

"Are the payments too much?" she said. "You can pay for it in 24 or 36 months."

Making payments on a vacuum. That sounds like the perfect definition of being financially overextended. "It's just that $2,100 is a lot for a vacuum," I said.

"And a shampooer," she reminded me, as if I could forget as she finished shampooing the carpet and the clock hit 10:00.

I told her to leave her number and we would think about it. But she wasn't leaving that easily. She picked up her cellular phone and called in reinforcements.

In walked Joe, her supervisor, who tried to wear us down with bold statements like, "You want to live in a clean house, right?" and "Are you mad that we showed you how much dirt there is in your home?"

Actually, I was just mad that it was 10:30 and somebody was in my house trying to sell me a vacuum that I never wanted.

Then Joe cut the price to $1,500, even though he said he would probably get in trouble with the boss. The price got down to $1,100 before Joe realized that I was happy with my "useless plastic vacuum." He left his phone number and left the house with the rest of the Kirby brigade.

Finally we were free, and at least the living-room carpet is now clean. But the dining room still needs some work. I think this week I'll call Joe and tell him he's won a major prize — an exciting second chance to convince me.

# Getting a feel for the phone-y deal

It's early in the evening and the time is right. It's time for coupon books that will add up to big savings, time for a special deal on a Hawaiian vacation and time for me to plan for my funeral expenses. It's time for me to get a great deal on a lovely pair of Teakwood shower clogs.

That's right, it's Telemarketer Prime Time.

Last night, Mr. Wizkon (I presume that's me) was awarded with a free subscription to two magazines. Apparently it was a reward for my good credit, or for being a loyal customer, or for that time when I was 8 years old and I was honest about eating the last popsicle. I really don't know why I was chosen for such a great honor. But I do remember that the magazines were absolutely free, except for the four-dollars-per-month processing fee.

I told the telemarketer that it truly was an exciting "free" offer and that I was overwhelmed by such a gracious reward, but unfortunately, I had never learned how to read.

"Do you have any audio books?" I asked.

That's how Mr. Wizkon, Mr. Wikskon and my other mangled pronunciations handle telemarketers. I learned it from my grandpa, who was the master of burning down a sales pitch. He was once offered a free dance lesson over the phone, and excitedly replied, "That's great, but I don't have any legs."

It's hard to live up to that, but I'm getting a lot of chances to practice because the telemarketing calls are increasing. That's not surprising, because believe it or not, the U.S. Constitution protects telemarketers' right to breed. That's reason enough to call your congressman.

I must admit, however, that I'm partly to blame for being the telemarketers' boy toy. I should have known that joining the "12 CDs for the price of one" compact disc club had a catch.

Does it ever. I think the club sold my name and number to every marketing company in the world. Now I spend my evenings turning down offers for troll collections, the "When Sharks Attack" video series, vinyl siding, and my favorite, Michael Jordan commemorative plates. Nothing captures the excitement of a basketball career like a dinner plate.

Unfortunately, I didn't have good comebacks for those sales pitches. But they'll call back. They always do. That's because telemarketers never cross anybody off a list, they just put you under the heading "Check back several times tomorrow."

That's why the same carpet-cleaning company called me for two weeks hoping that I would allow them to give me a free in-home demonstration. First they called for Matt Wixon, then Matthew Wixon, then Matthew P. Wixon, so I'm obviously on a lot of different lists. They finally asked for Matthew Wixon Jr., which made me wonder if there is a Matthew Wixon Sr. out there somewhere. Maybe I was adopted and my parents have been lying to me all these years.

Anyway, I finally gave in. After the fourth call from the cleaners, I agreed to let them come to my home for the demonstration.

"But don't come on Thursday," I said, "because that's when the cult meets. And how well does your cleaner work on goat hair and blood stains?"

They said they'd call me later. And as weird as it sounds, I'm sure they will.

# Swimming through a pool of deductions

Spring is here once again, the time when flowers begin to bud, birds sing sweetly and primal urges send men and women searching for that elusive joy in life — tax deductions.

Yes, the filing deadline is coming up fast, and everybody is looking for a way to ease the burden. That's why items unfit for a garage sale suddenly find great value when they are donated to charity.

Estimated value of my charitable donations this year? Well, I think the toaster that wouldn't leggo my Eggo is a bargain at $150, and the lamp that looks like a bowling pin is easily worth $200. As for the broken-down Huffy bike, I valued it at $750. It's 20 years old, so I think it gets the antique rate. It would've been more if it still had pedals.

Of course I'm joking, especially if you're one of those handsome and/or strikingly beautiful IRS agents reading this column (By the way, you sure look nice today!). The truth is, I realize that I live in a wonderful country, and it takes lots of money to keep it the best place in the world to live. And if taxpayers start shirking their responsibility, who will pay for the investigation of the president, space probes that forget to stop for directions and lawmakers who make crucial decisions like whether they want a shampoo with their free congressional haircut?

My vote is for Bill Gates. He can even e-file the money.

Unfortunately, that's not going to happen. So maybe we should just stop grumbling about taxes, appreciate what our government does for us and pay up. After all, this country does offer amazing opportunities, incredible freedoms, a high standard of living, and hey, wait a second, I *owe* the government $1,000? I thought I was getting a refund! Is the government funding another artist who plans to depict the despair of the world by sculpting Jell-O?

Maybe I need to go over my deductions and exemptions again. I must have missed something:

**DEPENDENTS:** My wife and I still don't have children, so we don't get much help here. But then again, I believe everyone needs to play a role in the upbringing of the world's children. I'll claim a couple of them.

**CAPITAL LOSSES:** I almost forgot my biggest capital loss of the year: 10,000 hair follicles. I've seen those Hair Club for Men commercials, and that club looks pretty pricey. A buck a follicle sounds fair.

**MOVING EXPENSES:** My new employer paid for these expenses, but several houseplants didn't survive the trip. And how can you put a price on the emotional attachment I had to them? I'll try. $2,000.

**BUSINESS EXPENSES:** Just as important as the pens, pencils, highlighters and erasers was the $472 for Cokes and $350 for chocolate-chip cookies from the vending machines. "If undersigned individual cannot operate without said sugar rush, whence lies his right to deduct said costs of tasty goodness." I'm pretty sure I read that somewhere.

**PAIN AND SUFFERING:** $1,000 for the pain of having to watch the machine malfunction and not give me the cookies. I'm adding $500 for suffering after I bruised my toe kicking the machine and another $500 for my emotional distress after noticing that somebody saw me kick it.

**GRATUITY:** I'll accept the customary 15 percent.

Now I'll crunch the new numbers on my calculator ($10 — business expense). Ah, that's much better. It looks like the government owes me $5,242, enough for the down payment on a pool.

All you IRS agents remember to bring your swim trunks for the audit.

# Home sweet home: Who will buy it?

Few things are more American than owning your own home. In fact, I'd rank it right up there with baseball, hot dogs, apple pie and the greatest American tradition — cholesterol-clogged arteries. But while owning your own home may be the American dream, buying the house, and even worse, selling it, can be an American nightmare.

I know this is hard for many of you to believe. That's because you've seen the realty commercials, where smiling buyers and sellers prove that the whole process is as easy as 1-2-3 — just before they dash to the next set to portray Excedrin Headache Sufferer No. 92.

Believe me, there is a step four. And it usually includes haggling over the price, fighting over closing costs and somebody getting hit upside the head with a For Sale sign. That's why so many of those signs are dented.

I know all this because I'm currently selling one house and buying another, making me the hunter and the hunted in the real estate game. It also allows me, according to real estate laws in all 50 states, to pretend that I know what I'm talking about.

I'll start with buying, since you can't sell anything until you buy it first, except in the case of your vital organs (a topic that will be addressed in my upcoming column "Selling a kidney on e-Bay for maximum profit").

Buying is the scariest part because you simply don't know what you're getting into. You don't know how well the owners took care of the house. You don't know how many years the roof will last. You don't know why there is a chalk outline of a body on the bedroom floor.

All you know is that everything you've dreamed of is way out of your price range, and everything you can afford looks like the gorilla habitat at the zoo. One house I toured recently had a huge grease stain across the carpet and a hole in the wall next to it. My guess is that the people who lived there decided a formal dining room wasn't as important as a formal test track for their Harley Davidson.

Not surprising, my real estate agent summed up the house the way she summed up every other house: "Perfect!" That's why I knew she was a great Realtor. The best agents can put a positive spin on anything that hasn't been condemned.

**The house is falling apart?** It's a handyman's dream!

**The landscaping is totally overgrown?** It's a gardener's delight!

**There is no roof?** It's a convertible!

Without a doubt, the exclamation point is the MVP of the real estate game. Some agents can't get through a whole sentence without one, as in: "Adorable! Gorgeous!! Includes attached roof!!!" The best agents, however, masterfully weave exclamation points with capital letters to create a mesmerizing description:

"CHARMER! LOADS OF POTENTIAL!! CONVERTED CRACKHOUSE!!!"

It can all be a little overwhelming for a buyer. It can also be depressing, because just when you think you've found the right house, in the right neighborhood, with owners that look like Ward and June Cleaver, you discover that the whole house is supported by termites holding hands.

So what is the savvy home-hunter to do?

It's simple: Buy from somebody you can trust. Buy from somebody who will be honest with you. Buy from a humor columnist who has an adorable three-bedroom house on the market right now.

IT'S PERFECT!!!

# Pull over, you're using the wrong fork

Somewhere in a dark room, the etiquette police is tearing down my performance the way Joan Rivers attacks an ill-fitting Versace dress on the Oscars' red carpet.

While enjoying a five-course meal in which everyone uses the correct utensils and properly folds their napkins, the etiquette authorities are breaking down the footage and piecing together a case that proves I am a cultural ape. They may even borrow the telestrator that excitable football broadcaster John Madden uses to diagram plays on television (Boom! Right there! He's using his salad fork to eat his strawberry cheesecake!)

Maybe it's just paranoia. Maybe the other guests at the wedding reception a few weeks ago didn't notice that I used the same fork for two separate courses. Maybe they were so focused on the happy bride and groom that they didn't notice my flagrant faux pas with the butter knife.

I hope so, because I admit I am not cultured. At least not in the art of fine dining. I grew up with a dad who liked to grill hamburgers and the number for Little Caesar's Pizza on speed dial. Finger foods were the rule — hot dogs, french fries, mashed potatoes.

OK, sometimes we used utensils. But I don't remember ever having a meal where one course's sole purpose was to cleanse the palate. And the wedding reception's dinner offered just that — a spoonful of sherbet in a kiwi to cleanse the palate. I knew this would be a tough assignment for Drive-Thru Man.

I had utensils everywhere. Spoons for dessert, stirring coffee and cleansing the palate. Forks for the main course, salad, wedding cake, and one with a purpose to be named later. It could've been for fending off opponents during the bouquet or garter toss, or maybe the extra fork was special to me in consideration of my ability to drop forks under the table.

That must be it. They had seen footage of my previous attempts at fine dining.

I had plenty of utensils, but what I really needed was plenty of napkins. The one napkin on my lap, which I neatly folded lengthwise to avoid a breach of etiquette, would not be enough if my tie decided to explore the gravy. And I figured it would eventually. That or my sleeve would land in butter, salad dressing would drop on my shirt, or — Doesn't everyone have nightmares like this? — when the meal is complete, I incorrectly place the knife with its sharp side facing *away* from the fork.

How embarrassing. The correct way to show you are finished with the meal, according to a dining etiquette guide provided by the Career Center at Ball State University, is as follows:

"Lay your fork diagonally across your plate. Place your knife and fork side by side, with the sharp side of the knife blade facing inward and the fork, tines down, to the left of the knife. The knife and fork should be placed as if they are pointing to the numbers 10 and 4 on a clock face."

But which end of the knife and fork should be facing toward the 10? Should the knife be on the left or the right? Should I insist that all of my dinnerware has clock faces on it?

For those of you asking the same questions, please join me in a basic etiquette class. We'll explore the elements of fine dining, including use of the soup spoon, proper ways to cut and eat your food, and why Martha Stewart has enough time to get eggs from her hen house, cut up tomatoes from her garden, make her own salsa and create a Spanish omelet that is shaped like Spain.

We'll cover everything in the etiquette class. And hopefully, along with your palate, it will cleanse any fears of your next brush with the upper crust. Make sure to bring lots of napkins.

# Now boarding frivolous shoppers

Flying in an airplane always makes me ponder the big questions in life. Zooming along helplessly at 20,000 feet, I ask: What is the meaning of life? Is there intelligent life on other planets? Given the popularity of Steven Seagal, would other planets consider Earth to have intelligent life?

Then the plane hits some turbulence. I suddenly realize that someone is painting their nails behind me, the guy next to me has taken off his shoes, and I still haven't received my bag containing nine honey-roasted peanuts. My oasis of meditation is interrupted, and I remember that I'm a weak swimmer in the pool of deep thought.

So with two hours left on my flight, I tackle questions more suited to my level of introspection, like "What person would buy a full suit of body armor?"

Apparently, people do. It's offered on page 169 of *Sky Mall* magazine, which I found in the seat pocket next to the air-sickness bag. "The 15th Century Full Suit of Armor is made in Italy using the same medieval smithing methods that were used in the 15th century to create the originals," the magazine says. And what a steal at just $2,450!

*Sky Mall* is full of exciting products. There's the most powerful nose-hair trimmer available ($39.95), a remote-controlled indoor triple-turbo blimp ($89.95) and "The Messaging Cap," which is $24.95.

The Messaging Cap looks like the hat Gilligan made famous, but with the addition of a programmable LCD display on the front. The magazine suggests programming messages such as "Go Team!" "What's your name?" or "To be or not to be, that is the question." I think the real question, given the failure rates at programming VCRs in this country, is "How many people would be walking around blinking 12:00?"

A clock that would never blink 12:00 is The World's Most Accurate Travel Alarm Clock ($39.95). The clock synchronizes itself with the U.S. Atomic Clock in Fort Collins, Colo., which means you'll never again have to rely on standard, inaccurate alarm clocks that can make you 27 seconds late for an important meeting.

For that meeting, you'll probably want the first-ever Digital Voice Recorder With Laser Pointer ($199.95). And to beef up the intellect in your presentation, how about developing a Harvard Graduate's Vocabulary in just 15 minutes a day? It's only $29.95 for the first two tapes, and it's been of proficious usufruct for this entire, indiscerptible sentence.

At the meeting you can hand out motivational tools from Successories, such as the Innovation poster ($89.99 framed). It has a photograph of a lightning strike, "INNOVATION" in big blue letters and this bit of wisdom: "The best way to predict the future ... is to create it." That is so true. And for the record, the worst way to predict the future is to call a 1-900 number.

Some of the other *Sky Mall* selections are The "Keep Your Distance" Insect Vacuum ($49.95), which lets you suck up those little suckers at an arm's length. There's also the body-heat watch ($119), The Street Flyers Roller Skate Shoes ($129.95) and the Neighborhood Bully Water Tormentor System ($29.99). That final product actually goes by a different name, and it's supposed to wash cars and driveways, but anyone who's taken a direct hit from a power sprayer knows that parental supervision isn't always available.

If you're looking for sweets, *Sky Mall* has a delicious selection of mail-order desserts ($39.95). And if you eat them all yourself, don't worry. Just order the Inch-Master ($29.50), which allows you to stretch the waist of cotton pants up to five inches.

Edging out the Inch-Master as my favorite product is the Nature Monitor ($39.95), which amplifies the sounds of nature outside your home so you can enjoy it in your mosquito-free living room. It sounds like a great way for me to relax, soothe my soul and strive for higher consciousness. Maybe then I can finally find answers to life's most perplexing questions.

And, of course, proudly display them on my Messaging Cap.

# Beekeeping or college: You make the call

Right now many people are considering going to college. Some are thinking about it as they blow off classes in high school, while others are thinking about it as they blow out 40 birthday candles before heading to work at Der Weinerschnitzel.

No matter what your age, my advice is to go for it. College is a ticket to ride toward a good career, and it was an extremely rewarding experience for me. Well, except for the 35 times I walked down my dorm's fire escape during a 3 a.m. fire alarm. And there was my first roommate, who played wargames all day and didn't take showers, and I'll never forget the lines at the bookstore ...

Anyway, the point is that you *should* go to college. And the first thing you need to do is find the right college for you. But with so many choices these days, it's not easy to find a cushy niche where you can experience the world of higher learning and shrinking bank accounts.

Well, here's a tip: You can avoid wasting time by narrowing your list of college choices. Many universities are even courteous enough to help you do this.

"Mr. Wixon, thank you for applying to Princeton! We are honored to inform you that you will be admitted to the university as soon as we lower our standards."

My final list included the University of Arizona, Arizona State University, the University of Southern California and a mail-order study program endorsed by Sally Struthers. Making the final decision was tough, especially considering how enthusiastic Sally was about the welding, TV/VCR repair and beekeeping courses.

I decided on the University of Arizona, where 35,000 students work, play and occasionally stay conscious on weekends. And I don't regret it for a minute, because unlike many other colleges and universities, I was not just a number to the U of A. Nope, I was a combination of numbers and letters.

I believe I was AD47523416. Let me check, it's tattooed on my arm.

OK, I'm kidding about that. But I'm not kidding about finding the right school. That's why it's very important to get input from people who have gone to the school that interests you. They can tell you about campus life, which professors are the best and how to set up an intervention for a roommate who plays wargames all day and doesn't take showers.

Even more important, your collegiate elders can tell you which classes will make the drive to a degree a little smoother.

A tip by a friend led me to a paranormal anthropology class that counted as a social sciences credit. In the class, I learned about auras, psychic abilities and watched a guy, allegedly, communicate with the dead. I also had my palm read, and the reader revealed that I would get an "A" on the final if I studied.

What a revelation!

A second revelation, thanks to another tip, was how I could get my fine arts credit by taking "Theatre Appreciation." The students in this class, most of which could bench press 350 pounds or scrape their heads on the top of the doorways, were required to attend plays and then review a certain element of each, like the lighting, the acting, or my choice, the candy selection at the concession stand. It was a slam-dunk credit, perfect for several of my classmates who are now in the NBA.

If you're getting the idea that choosing the right college is much harder than college itself, you're right. The only really tough decision in college is what to major in, and that gets easier as time goes by. I know my last four majors were fairly easy decisions.

So nobody should be afraid of college. And I can assure you that the years of cramming for finals, writing 3,000 word essays on Eastern European political thought and stealing the pieces to your roommate's wargames will pay off. You'll be rewarded with a diploma, which I display next to my beekeeping certificate signed by Sally Struthers.

I feel proud reading both of them, but especially my diploma:

In accordance with his completion of all the requirements, The University of Arizona on this day bestows a BACHELOR'S DEGREE in JOURNALISM to AD47523416.

I'm glad they spelled my name right.

# My old friend keeps trying to cash in

Over the years, I've lost contact with most of my friends from college. In the case of my buddy, Milo, who spent an entire year playing Nintendo and dropping classes, some distance is a good thing.

But I regret that I let so many other friends slip away. I miss them sometimes, along with my exciting, carefree, full-head-of-hair college days. The days when I strove for greater knowledge by investigating theories, challenging widely held beliefs and limiting myself to two presses of the snooze bar. (The first 20 minutes of Introduction to British Literature weren't that important).

Despite the pull of time and geography, however, I have kept in touch with one friend. Actually, it's more like one friend has kept in touch with me. Every few months, this friend calls to check on how my life is going and how my job is working out. And, of course, whether I can spare some extra change.

"Milo, is that you?"

No, it's not the Nintendo wonder boy. It's my old buddy the University of Arizona, who as a student, I affectionately called "The U." (In return, The U. affectionately referred to me as "Student No. AD47523416." It was something like that, anyway, because I remember that I was not just a number to The U. — I was a combination of numbers and letters.)

Anyway, last week The U. called me up for a few minutes of reminiscing and begging. According to The U. representative, it was a "friendly" call that the university likes to make to alumni.

It started out friendly. We talked about the university's expanded computer labs and new student union. We talked about my approaching 10-year reunion. We even talked about the basketball team's great season and how half the players turned pro after the final game.

It was fun to talk about college again, especially because I really loved the University of Arizona and the whole college experience. And as I told stories of getting lost in the social sciences building, changing my major four times and standing in line for three hours to get a student ID card, it felt like I was talking to an old friend.

But along with hairlines and waistlines, it seems time changes friendships. After a few minutes, I realized The U. and I had grown in different directions. While I still wanted to swap stories about 3 a.m. fire drills in the dormitories, my buddy started talking about capital improvements, funding shortfalls and donor levels.

Granted, I think about money a lot more than 10 years ago. These days I'm more likely to view an exciting CD opportunity as a certificate of deposit than the latest release from R.E.M. But while The U. and I share a heightened interest in my money, we have a serious problem: I'm concerned about keeping it, whereas The U. wants a piece of it. That's not a healthy recipe for a friendship.

So our talk turned serious. The U. representative suddenly began talking like an insurance salesman concerned about my level of collision coverage.

He talked about the crucial role of alumni. He mentioned the "gold level" and becoming a "partner" with the university. I tuned out after that, but phrases like "one thousand dollars, two thousand or more" and "payment plans" came up several times.

"Alumni like you are essential," I remember him saying. "The university is counting on your continued support."

Continued support? My friend doesn't know me very well. Other than a few basketball tickets and a couple of U of A sweatshirts, I haven't funded The U. since I received my diploma. Extending payments to the school after my graduation hasn't even been tempting.

So I declined to make a donation — again. But I know our friendship isn't over. The U. will call again soon for another "friendly" chat. And when my buddy asks me to continue my current support levels, I might have some good news:

I've got my eye on a new Arizona baseball cap.

# A feast of thanks to glue us together

This week children around the country are learning about Thanksgiving in school. They're making pilgrim hats, drawing a turkey using the outline of their hand and holding their own Thanksgiving feast — with traditional Thanksgiving foods like Tootsie Rolls, Sweet Tarts and Elmer's School Glue. They're also listing the things they are thankful for, like their moms and dads, their Pokemon card collection and the upcoming release of the Mortal Kombat game where you can tear a guy's head off and the blood looks totally real.

It sure is cute, the kids being so naive about it all. It will be years before they truly appreciate the reasons to give thanks in this country, where we have the right to life, liberty and the pursuit of as many cable channels as possible, including the 24-hour aquarium network.

For now, the kids are learning about the first Thanksgiving, which many people believe never happened. But as the story goes, Thanksgiving started when the pilgrims and the indians first shared a feast, sometime between the Greco-Prussian War and the War of the Worlds. It was an important event because the pilgrims and indians sat down together for a time of peace, understanding, and of course, pro football. Records indicate that the whole day was sponsored by Budweiser.

It was a festive time filled with laughter, joy, and most importantly, a hope for an enduring peace. Unfortunately, the peace ended the next day — the busiest shopping day of the year — when a battle began over the last Furby at Macy's.

That's how I remember it, anyway. But I guess my memory

isn't one of the things I'm thankful for. I do, however, have many reasons to be thankful this year.

For example, I am thankful for the members of my family who don't greet me by saying "Where has all your hair gone?" or "Do you know that you're losing your hair?" Of course, this doesn't really bother me because I have such a positive attitude about hair loss, and more important, a nice collection of hats.

Here's the rest of my list, which I believe is almost as good as my turkey drawing from back in second grade:

- I am thankful for my wonderful wife, even if she enjoys finding my new gray hairs. (Again, this isn't a problem, because I have a positive attitude about the whole hair thing, dammit.)
- I am thankful for my two dogs, who bravely defend the house from threats like the mailman, 7-year-olds on bikes and plastic bags blowing in the wind.
- I am thankful that all the airlines say they are Y2K ready, and even more thankful that I will not be flying in an airplane on New Year's Eve.
- I am thankful that, for the first time in months, I don't have a song from a Gap commercial running through my head.
- I am thankful that some teenagers still do not carry pagers.
- I am thankful that I'm often mistaken for Brad Pitt.
- I am thankful that the readers of this column, as well as Brad Pitt, will understand that the writer may occasionally stray from the facts in an attempt to keep a positive attitude about the whole hair issue, dammit.
- I am thankful for all the compassionate people of this world who are a friend to everyone and spend their lives helping those in need. I am thankful that I still have time to try to be one of these people.
- Most important, I am thankful that Elmer's School Glue is non-toxic.

# Here we come a caroling: Lock your doors

First of all, thanks to everyone for joining this year's caroling group. It's great to know that even in the rush of the holidays, we can take time to share the spirit of the season with our neighbors. And please give a special welcome to Bob, who has made it out here despite his recent illness. By the way, Bob thanks everyone for their prayers and says his recent bout with trichinosis taught him the glory of God and the importance of properly preparing the Thanksgiving turkey.

If you don't know me, I'm Mrs. Mayberry, and I teach music at the local elementary school. But please don't be intimidated by my musical ability, which is a combination of natural talent — Praise God! — and years of diligent training. Be assured that I will not criticize the efforts of any of you musical beginners as we spread the joy of the season, unless you hit each other with song flutes like those heathens in the third grade.

I have just a few more announcements before we get started. We all know that David, one of our most devoted singers of the past few years, won't be with the group this year. But with your prayers, I believe his unfortunate incarceration will end soon. And in light of his arrest, I remind you that although the lyrics of "We Wish You a Merry Christmas" say that we won't go until we get some Figgie pudding, we *will* go if a restraining order is slapped on us. That's also why we won't be sharing holiday harmonies this season with 4704 Juniper Boulevard.

I know it's cold out here, but just a few more notes before we croon our happy tune. Sadly, we have lost one of our caroling sponsors this season, Aunt Jemima Syrup. That means there will not be a pancake dinner after tonight's singing. But it also means that, for the first time in three years, we can sing "Here We Come a Wassailing" instead of "Here We Come a Waffling."

Our first song, however, will be in salute to our longtime sponsor:

*"We wish you a merry Christmas,*
*"We wish you a merry Christmas,*
*"We wish you a merry Christmas,*
*"From Budweiser Beer!"*

And the second song will be for our newest sponsor, Fran's Fall Fashions, which graciously donated the scarves that are keeping us all warm tonight:

*"Hark the herald angels sing,"*
*"50 percent off everything,"*
*"Peace on earth and mercy mild,"*
*"Check Fran's sales, you'll go wild."*

After those two songs, we are free to give glory to God by raising our voices. And remember, we are all God's children, and everyone's voice is beautiful in the ears of God. In the ears of humans, however, some voices are the equivalent of fingernails scraping on a chalkboard. In that case, please give glory to God by simply moving your lips to the words.

And speaking of words, we need to clarify a few lyrics that were incorrect last year. In "The Christmas Song" — the song that starts "Chestnuts roasting on an open fire" — there seems to be some confusion. The correct lyrics are "later on, we'll conspire, as we sit by the fire," instead of, "later on, we'll perspire, as we sit by the fire." I understand the confusion, but I don't think underarm wetness should have a place in our caroling.

As for the other song with incorrect lyrics, I think it's more childishness than confusion. Last year I heard many people tainting the beautiful "Walking in a Winter Wonderland" with the words, "walking 'round in women's underwear." That kind of immaturity won't help us share the warmth of the season, and I simply won't allow it.

Unless Victoria's Secret wants to sponsor us and help pay David's legal fees.

# Holidays: Great cheer and fabulous fiction

Julie is a gorgeous young woman attending the University of Smartypants and is at the top of her class. John is a strapping young fellow who all the girls are chasing after. Billy is only 5 years old, but we're pretty sure he's a genius.

Sounds a lot like a list of characters from the latest show on the WB network, especially if Julie is always wearing spandex. But no, it's one of those holiday letters many people like to include with their Christmas cards.

Any day now, I'll get one. Some friend or relative will send a holiday greeting in the most personal way possible: a typed letter. Typed, of course, because that's the easiest way to send out a million of them.

They start with "Happy Holidays!" and end with "Hope you have a great year!" but it's really about "Hey, look at me!"

A brag letter.

And boy do they have plenty to brag about.

For these people, who send out Xeroxed breakdowns of their year to everyone from close friends to people they run into with their shopping cart, every year is worth bronzing. It's always been an exceptional year — the lords are leaping, the swans are swimming and the ladies are dancing finer than ever.

The letters are best when parents are writing about their children. That's when the fiction flies most furiously.

One son is an inventor, while another is really cleaning up during the boom on Wall Street. And they're so proud of their daughter, who's devoting her time to troubled relationships.

What they don't tell you is that the one son's only invention is a new improved burp, the other is cleaning toilets on Wall Street and the daughter is the booking agent for *Jerry Springer*.

It also seems something big always gets left out of the letter.

Hmm. I'm suspicious. Could it be they just forgot to mention the other daughter, the one whose only goal was to attend every Mariah Carey concert?

And what about the father's unfortunate run-in with the intern at work? (I'm assuming that was cut from the Clintons' letter).

Now I know that some news just doesn't fit the holiday spirit. But growing up, I thought I was falling way behind. According to the holiday brag letters, the children of my parents' friends and relatives were turning the world upside down while I was turning up the volume on *The Brady Bunch*.

I mean, I was 14 years old and I still hadn't written my first book. What a loser.

I wish my parents would've fought back with similar letters. With just the right spin, my teen-age career could've been described as news director. After all, it was news that I was throwing, and I did direct it toward people's driveways.

And in the Wixon brag letter, my brother could've been working in the exciting, fast-paced world of retail food. In fact, he could've been described as vice president of drive-thru.

Such a missed opportunity for some fabulous fiction.

That's why I'm working on my brag letter:

"Happy Holidays! Yes, it's been a great year for my family. I'm devilishly handsome, my wife's just getting more gorgeous, and together we virtually run the state of Texas.

All the flowers are blooming and all of the birds are chirping on the acres surrounding our fabulous estate. Hope you have a great year!"

But make sure you call before you visit.

# Dazzling rarely comes at a discount

I hate to interrupt your tidings of comfort and joy during this season of special holiday hours and fruitcake paperweights, but it's my duty to report some very un-jolly information.

The price of Christmas gifts has gone up again.

No kidding, you say. The price of Christmas gifts goes up every year. Does this columnist think I'm a moron?

Hey, I just report the news, I don't make it up. I swear to it on my *Guidebook to Journalistic Ethics*, which is personally signed by the author, Geraldo Rivera.

It's true, the information on gift prices was really on the news. Granted, it was the radio news — and they were broadcasting from a huge inflatable radio at the grand opening of a Dunkin' Donuts — but it was still the news. And according to the report, everything from Anorexia Barbie to Annoy Me Elmo will be pricier this year.

Even the cost of "The 12 Days of Christmas" is up. Yep, this year you'll have to dish out $59,000 to give your true love everything from the 12 drummers drumming to the partridge in a pear tree. That price does not include shipping, handling or legal fees resulting from stuffing nine ladies dancing into a UPS box.

This was crushing news for me, since I had already rounded up the four calling birds, three french horns (couldn't find hens) and two turtle doves for my true love. But it appears that I can only afford the four days of Christmas.

Then again, maybe I can get a better deal than the researchers. I don't know how they came up with the $59,000 figure, anyway. I mean, just where do you go to buy eight maids-a-milking?

I'll bet they didn't get the best prices. Sure, you can pick up 11 pipers piping and 10 lords-a-leaping at any department store, but did they shop around?

Did they use double coupons? Did they check the Home Shopping Network? I think I saw the piping pipers and leaping lords as a package deal on there, right after the Cooking King Miracle Chopper-Slicer-Manicure set.

Of course, most of us are not eccentric millionaires with housekeepers to clean up after the seven swans-a-swimming and six geese-a-laying. Most of us have a hard time buying gifts without decking the halls with credit card receipts.

It's even worse for men. Jewelry commercials say our wives will leave us if we don't get them something dazzling for the last Christmas of the Millennium. I ask you: Are fuzzy slippers no longer considered dazzling?

It all makes me long for my childhood, when anything I made with my crayons and glue was the most precious gift ever. But while an 8-year-old giving love for Christmas is considered beautiful, a 28-year-old doing the same is considered a sign of a serious disorder.

That's what we call the modern spirit.

Too bad I can no longer shop at the Horizon Elementary School Holiday Gift Shop. That was the perfect place for an 8-year-old to get all his shopping done, during school hours no less, and for just five dollars. A football eraser for my brother, a glitter pen for my sister and a coffee mug for my dad ran me only three bucks. That left me with two dollars left for my big purchase, a #1 Mom necklace.

Without question, it was dazzling.

# Saint Nick: The definitive interview

With a little old driver so lively and quick, I knew in a moment it must be Saint Nick.

On the phone, that is.

Yes, in what I believe is an exclusive interview, I spoke with Santa Claus recently. He agreed to speak with me as long as I kept it short, which I assured him wouldn't be a problem since the nickel-a-minute rate doesn't include calls to the North Pole.

**Q:** Well, the big night is almost here. I'm sure things are pretty exciting up there, eh Santa?

**SANTA:** Yes, it is pretty hectic here. Whether it's preparing the sleigh, trying to find all my gift lists or finalizing flight plans, there's always something more to do. And I always forget something. One year I forgot my belt and had to make a quick flyback because I couldn't keep my darn pants up. Especially on Christmas Eve, I wanted to make sure there was just one moon in the sky, you know what I mean?

**Q:** Of course. Are there any other problems?

**SANTA:** Well, the reindeer always have a problem. Dancer isn't dancin', Prancer isn't prancin' or Rudolph's schnoz has an electrical problem. I'm not even sure if Comet will be able to streak on Christmas Eve because he's got a lingering hoof injury from a rough landing a year ago.

**Q:** Wow, so there really is trouble sometimes. We just wake up, see the stockings filled and assume everything went well. We figure that because you are a saint, you have the right people on your side.

**SANTA:** Yes, but even a saint has trouble delivering presents all over the world in one night. I do have secrets, but there have been a few times when ol' Santa almost didn't make it. One time long ago, before seatbelts, airbags and anti-lock brakes, I had a bad accident. It was in your part of the country, as a matter of fact. I tried to land in a grassy field, which is pretty darn tricky in a sleigh built for snow, crashed hard and got thrown clear of the sleigh. I couldn't remember my name for a few minutes, but I did finish the route.

**Q:** You didn't happen to run over an old lady on that trip, did you?

**SANTA:** If you're referring to that song "Grandma Got Run Over by a Reindeer," I can tell you that's a big sham. I have never hurt anyone but myself.

**Q:** Well, it has to be exhausting. Traveling all around the world year after year, not even factoring in the accidents. You must be in better shape than you appear to be.

**SANTA:** Just what do you mean by that?

**Q:** I'm sorry. I didn't mean anything bad. But you know how the famous poem goes: "He had a round little belly that shook when he laughed like a bowl full of jelly."

**SANTA:** I've always found that a little offensive. You know, it's not easy to get washboard abs when people are putting milk and cookies out for you. And I'm not really fat, I'm just big-boned.

**Q:** You don't have to prove anything to me, Santa. But some people aren't so crazy about you because you don't fit into the true meaning of Christmas. You know, Jesus is the reason for the season.

**SANTA:** Well, the way I see it, Christmas has different meanings for different people. It's a religious holiday, yes, but not everybody is Christian. I love all people, however, and all people can try to be nice to one another and care for one another. That's what I'm all about. That's why, when I drive out of sight, I can wish Merry Christmas to *all*.

**Q:** And to all a good night?

**SANTA:** Hey, that's my line.

# Working vacation? What a Presidential idea

By now, President Bush's brain-to-mouth train wreck is common knowledge. His mispronunciation of subliminal as "subliminable" was a classic, and he topped it when he told a group of workers, "I know it's hard to put food on your families."

So our president isn't good with words. And yes, some phrases shoot right over his head. He also gives pained expressions when deciphering sentences more complex than, "If dumb was dirt, he'd cover about an acre."

But even if we can deny the brilliance of George W. Bush, we can't deny his courage. Can anyone deny the courage it takes to leave a job for a month and call it a "working vacation"?

That's how Bush is explaining his monthlong stay at his ranch in Texas. I think it's worth a medal for bravery, or at least a reminder that a good portion of the American people are smarter than him.

A working vacation? That's harder to picture than Bush and Saddam Hussein in a warm embrace. I expect that when the month is over, someone will ask about a proposed law and Bush will say, "I remember reading some papers about that, but I think they blew out of the golf cart on the 15th hole."

To give Bush some credit, he did make a decision on federal funding of stem-cell research. I, underestimating the leader of the free world, guessed that he would wait until the end of the working vacation and announce, "I was really close to making up my mind, but then I sat in the jacuzzi for 30 minutes and forgot what I was thinking about."

What I won't forget is this working vacation idea. I don't buy it for a second, but like most people, I'm willing to try it. And I figure that if the President says this is OK, surely I can get it by my boss, one of the hardest-working, snappy-dressing, brilliant-idea, open-to-columnists-taking- suspicious-vacations bosses in the universe.

First up will be a trip to Hawaii to investigate the overcommercialization of the popular vacation spot. It could take weeks to really flesh out a column on that topic. And what about the erosion of the beaches? I'm willing to hang out there as long as it takes to write a good column about such an important subject. I'll even talk to some of the locals if they bring me a mai tai.

Next, I'll take a trip to Europe to get insight on the world's image of the United States. What does Italy think of the routine bombings of Iraq? Does England think our President is as sharp as a mashed potato? Is Germany offended by Der Weinerschnitzel restaurants?

Finally, I'll tackle an issue that affects everyone: the energy crisis. This will require stops in major cities throughout the United States. San Francisco, Seattle, Miami, New York, Chicago — those seem to be reasonable places to survey gas prices, get the mood of the people and send postcards to my friends. While I'm in New York, I'll also need some tickets to Broadway shows. Hey, who doesn't need a little vacation from their working vacation?

My boss might not like the idea, but at least the President will understand. And I'm sure that because my trips are part of a *working* vacation, it won't alarm him when I claim any money I spend on these trips as business expenses.

I plan to be as productive as our President, so I think denying me the business expenses would be wrong. In the words of the leader of the free world, it might even be criminable.

# The reality is, 'Survivor' sucked us in

Since we started watching these people build shelter, eat rats, get bitten by bugs and plot strategy to stab each other in the back, one question has been buzzing in the minds of Americans:

Can't we do something to help the mentally ill?

Well maybe, but not right now, because *Survivor* is on!

And last week a bazillion people tuned in, give or take a few gazillion, to watch the final episode of the CBS reality series. That's because for months the suspense has mounted as faithful viewers wondered, with a million dollars on the line, which marooned competitor would kill the annoying host first. Sadly, it turned out that the host survived, making the last episode less satisfying than a rice cake and Diet Coke.

But at least *Survivor* is over for this season. No longer do we have to watch the competitors run through obstacle courses to gain "immunity" at the tribal council. No longer do we have to watch them roll in mud to win a challenge and be rewarded with a Budweiser (the official beer of *Survivor*), an Ericsson mobile phone (the official phone of *Survivor*), or a pair of Dr. Scholl's insoles (the official shoe-cushioning product of *Survivor*). Most important, as the official complaint source of *Survivor*, I no longer have to whine about the show I watched every week.

Yes, I got hooked by *Survivor*. I'm not proud of it, except that by contributing to the success of the show I probably kept the next masterpiece of Aaron Spelling — the genius behind *Fantasy Island* and *Beverly Hills: 90210* — off the air. Maybe Spelling's next show could maroon the *90210* cast on *Fantasy Island* and we could all vote to keep them there.

Anyway, now that we all know the final survivor, we can move on. And it's not a moment too soon, because presidential candidates George W. Bush and Al Gore are revving up their campaigns and Americans need to focus on what is really important, like who will be the winner on *Big Brother*.

That's right, the other CBS reality show is still on the air, and it's gaining popularity. Last week an exciting episode featuring the housemates sitting on the couch, then lying on the couch, and finally standing by the couch, beat out several shows from the UPN network and an infomercial for the newest breakthrough in fitness technology, the Torso Track. I can only imagine the ratings next week, when the *Big Brother* cameras capture the housemates cleaning the toilets with the official toilet cleaner of *Big Brother*.

*Big Brother* was hyped as landmark television because it features a small house filled with cameras to capture the occupants' every move. Unfortunately, in the first seven weeks of the show, they haven't moved very much. But at least from a sociological standpoint, we've learned that if you put 10 normal people together in a small house, film their every move and pit them against each other for a $500,000 prize, the result is a television show nearly as thrilling as a volume of the Encyclopedia Britannica.

And although I don't expect it to be part of the PBS lineup anytime soon, *Survivor* was also educational. We learned about treaties, vendettas and the value of building relationships. And we should all learn a valuable lesson from Richard, the castaway who was the ringleader of the group.

After seven weeks deserted on an island, he's still overweight. Either someone was smuggling him some Dolly Madison or nutritionists are wrong and a diet of fish and rice really isn't that healthy.

Maybe the next *Survivor* series should be sponsored by the Torso Track.

# Compelling, shocking, unforgettable, read on

Well, the *Who Wants to Marry a Multimillionaire?* marriage didn't work out, and it was just plain heartbreaking to see such a sweet couple split up. The way he longingly reached for her hand as she longingly reached for his wallet, I really thought that this rich-boy-who-allegedly-threatened-to-kill-a-former-girlfriend-meets-girl-who-he-picked-from-50-money-hungry-contestants story might work out. But maybe I'm just a hopeless romantic.

Anyway, although the marriage isn't working out, it did earn Fox some huge ratings. And this is the perfect time to reel in viewers, because we're in a "sweeps" period, when all the networks sweep up their best programming, throw it in the trash and broadcast yet another version of the JonBenet Ramsey story.

By the way, don't tell me how it ends. I'm taping it.

The sweeps period is important to the networks because it helps set the prices for commercial time after the sweeps period, when the networks return to regularly scheduled reruns. That's why the competition is so fierce right now, and why the networks are promoting their shows so heavily:

"This week on an unforgettable *ER*, a story so shocking and compelling that it truly is must-see television as many shocking things happen in a very compelling manner that you will find unforgettable. ..."

"This week on an unforgettable *Dateline*, Stone Phillips brings you a shocking interview with JonBenet Ramsey's parents in a way so compelling that you will find it unforgettable. ..."

"Next week on yet another unforgettable *ER*, the doctors jump into action after the Ramseys stab Stone Phillips during a compelling interview that turns into an unforgettable emergency that is truly must-see TV."

Again, please don't tell me how it ends. I'm taping it.

All of this craziness started back in 1926, when John Logie Baird first introduced television to the public. A few people were chosen to join him in his London lab to watch the first television broadcast: an unforgettable, compelling show featuring blurry lines, a screen full of white static and commercials with lawyers that promised to "fight for you!"

The next day, this historic statement was released to the media:

"BAIRD TELEVISION WINS IN ALL KEY DEMOGRAPHIC GROUPS, INCLUDING WOMEN 18-34, MEN 25-45 AND FRIENDS OF JOHN LOGIE BAIRD."

Obviously, it was an overwhelming success. But today, increased competition makes it much more difficult to win all the demographic groups. There are the regular networks, plus cable, plus many people now like to spend their free time in more rewarding ways than watching television, such as helping out at a retirement home, volunteering in a community improvement project or downloading pictures of Pamela Anderson Lee off the Internet.

So the networks have to be a little outrageous, as well as overdramatic. For example, it's not enough for the networks to call their made-for-television movies "world premiere movies." They promote each as a "world premiere movie EVENT." This apparently makes the movies more unforgettable, not to mention compelling. Oh yes, and shocking, too — I'm always leaving one of those adjectives out.

But the biggest trick of the television trade is the cliffhanger. There's simply no better way to bring viewers back for another week during the sweeps than a "To Be Continued." It's annoying, however, and unfair to viewers who can't see the show the following week because they are busy working at the retirement home, where they are using the computer to e-mail pictures of Pamela Anderson Lee to their friends.

Of course, what I've told you is just the tip of the iceberg. The television networks have many more tricks. So be sure to tune in next week for part two of this shocking, compelling, unforgettable column event.

# Watch out for scams, and check out this offer

Whenever I'm wrestling with one of life's tough questions, I head for my favorite thinking place: the return line at Wal-Mart. You have to watch out for those falling prices — was $4.99, now $4.97! — but the line gives you plenty of time to cerebrate and cogitate (or just plain think if you weren't returning a thesaurus like I was).

It's a long wait because somebody in front of me is always trying to pull a fast one. The last time I was there, a guy was trying to return a pair of jeans with holes in both knees that he swears he bought a week ago.

"I washed them once and this happened!" he says. "And no, I don't have the receipt because it was in the pocket while I washed them."

What a scam artist.

But I guess we all have a little bit of scam artist in us. Sure, we put up a good front. But no matter how many times we bake cookies for the church social and help little old ladies across the street, we're still fast-talking encyclopedia salesmen in the fine print of our lives.

Unfortunately, it's human nature. That's why we keep hearing more and more about people getting scammed, and not just by the Publisher's Clearing House "You may already be a loser!" Sweepstakes.

The scariest part is that we're all vulnerable these days, not just the little old lady you helped across the street so she could pay $42,000 for a new air conditioner. The good news is that you can minimize your risk by getting educated on the topic.

And thankfully, I have written a book that will help you do just that. It's guaranteed to answer all of your questions about scams, which makes it a real value at any price. But today you can order it by sending me just $50.**

**Supplies are limited. Guarantee does not apply to people who have too many questions. "Real value" in no way implies that book is either real or a value. Book may or may not be sent to you. Book may or may not have words.

Some of you might not have the $50 to spend, which I understand completely. Maybe it's because you got taken by a scam and no longer have that kind of spendable income.

Now that's a sad commentary on our society. It distresses me that anyone would cheat another person in that way. But like I wrote earlier, this is the way of the world. So to help you get the $50 for the indispensable book (which by the way is fully guaranteed and still available), I have created a wealth-building system that is guaranteed to end all of your money worries. And the best part is that, as a Special Bonus to help you get back on your feet, the wealth-building program is now on sale for half price!

Just send me $25 and I will rush you the information.##

##Supplies are limited. "Sale" does not imply that product was ever sold at full price. "Special Bonus" does not suggest that product is in any way a bonus or special. Terms and conditions of guarantee may change without notice. You may gain or lose money. You may already be a winner.

If you can't afford the wonderful wealth-building system, I do understand. It's just $25, but times are tough and each one of us is different. Some of us may decide that it's more important to save 25 bucks than pursue our dreams.

In that case, I just hope that you've learned something from this column. After all, that's the real reason I'm writing it. Well, that and to promote my spectacular sale going on now. I'm offering a great deal on a pair of jeans. They have fashionable patches on the knees, and I only wore them once.$$

$$Author bears no responsibility for accuracy of statements. Use of word "learn" in no way implies that above column is

educational. Use only as directed. Consult a physician before starting any exercise program. Your mileage may vary.

# Lordy mercy! Y'all should visit Texas

As an official, honest-to-goodness resident of Big Hat Country, I'm starting this column off with a big Hooooow-deeeee!

OK, so I've been in Dallas less than a week. But I already love it here, even if it's hotter than "whoopee in woolens."

That's Texas slang for dang hot. Others prefer to say "it's as hot as a billy goat in a pepper patch," whatever that means. Yes, it will take some time to get used to the lingo.

But Dallas isn't nearly as strange as I was prepared for.

"You're moving to Dallas? Man, that's the South," a friend told me, in a show of support I truly appreciated. "They wear boots. They like the Cowboys. And worst of all, everybody there is y'all this and y'all that."

Well, I tell y'all, Dallas really isn't that different from Phoenix. Sure, there are a lot more people and a lot less cacti, but just like in Arizona, there's an Applebee's restaurant five minutes from my house. Actually, it seems like there are about 17 of them.

So Walt Disney was right. It *is* a small world after all, even when you're not on a slow-moving boat begging wooden figurines to stop singing.

The scariest part about Dallas was getting here, especially with a pair of yapping, small-bladdered dogs as cargo. I'm still surprised that our two-car caravan stayed together. I tend to hold up the slow lane, whereas my wife has a heavier foot than a mob squealer thrown in the Hudson River.

(Note: In an effort to be fair, I'll add that my wife calls that accusation "preposterous." She would also like to point out that she doesn't have that many speeding tickets.)

Thankfully, we made it without casualties, other than a thousand or so insects that merged with our windshields. Now we're spending time checking out the city, looking at maps and getting more confused than a goat on Astroturf.

See how well I'm fitting in! That's a little more regional slang for you. I know I won't be using it very often, however. I also won't be wearing cowboy boots, eating grits or ordering a McPossum Value Meal.

I may be living in the South, after all, but I grew up in Phoenix. I've never eaten butterbeans, owned a cowboy hat or known anyone named "Bubba."

And trying to change me now would be like puttin' socks on a rooster. I mean Lordy Mercy! If you think you can, you must be an idiot. If your brains were ink, you couldn't dot an i.

No, I won't change, even if I'm as welcome in Dallas as a porcupine at a nudist colony. That may sound like I believe the sun rises just to hear me crow, but I have to be me. To be somebody that I'm not would be like being on a first-name basis with the bottom of the deck. And that's never a good idea, just like frying bacon naked.

So my new neighbors will just have to take me as I am. And I think they will, because show 'nuff, I'm fixin' to do some great things here in the beautiful city of Dallas. One of those great things will be to continue writing for you folks in the ol' West. And I'm sure you'll be able to tell it's the same old me, just coming from a different hitchin' post.

But for now, it's time to put out the fire and call in the dogs. I've got one wheel down and the axle draggin', and if I don't get some sleep, I might get a hitch in my git-along. And y'all know that would make it hard for me to just be me.

# This column flunked the drug test

In the great tradition of investigative journalism, I am writing this column while using a performance-enhancing drug. That's right, I'm hopped up on pseudoephedrine, a substance banned by the International Olympic Committee.

It's also an ingredient in NyQuil, the sniffling, sneezing, coughing, aching, take-it-and-stick-your-dismount-after- three-flips-off-the-parallel-bars medicine.

I didn't know about that last benefit, but apparently it's true. Last week Romanian gymnast Andreea Raducan was stripped of her gold medal because she took cold medicine that contained pseudoephedrine, which the IOC considers a performance-enhancing drug. And clearly, Raducan's performance in the all-around competition was enhanced by the pseudoephedrine. I talked to several gymnastics experts this week, and they all agreed that Raducan's scores would have been much lower if she had stopped in the middle of her routines to wipe her nose.

But what other advantage did the 16-year-old get from pseudoephedrine? That's hard to tell, and that's why I am on pseudoephedrine right now. I need to know the true performance-enhancing qualities of this drug. I also hope it will enhance my writing so that I can challenge for a medal in speed sarcasm, which I believe has as much right to be an Olympic event as trampolining or synchronized diving. Somehow they got into the Olympics.

So far the results of my pseudoephedrine study are mixed. I can report that my eyes are neither itchy nor watery, and I am not coughing. Clear nasal passages also seem to be enhancing my performance, but I'm still struggling with my tumbling passes on the floor exercise.

Here's something else I'm struggling with. How do we

determine what substances are illegally performance-enhancing? Steroids — Yes, I understand how they are performance-enhancing, both to the athletes and the financial portfolios of pro wrestling organizations. But what about the other performance-enhancing drugs that are not banned?

Aspirin relieves pain in joints, obviously enhancing performance. Tylenol reduces fever, obviously enhancing performance. And if you're spelling relief R-O-L-A-I-D-S, aren't you really spelling "cheat"? A person suffering from heartburn is obviously not going to perform as well as someone who has found an unnatural way to deal with acid reflux. It could be a huge advantage, if you believe all the commercials where a serious-looking actor, portraying a doctor, talks about the world's desperate need for fast heartburn relief.

And what about the many drugs that were advertised during the Olympics? The prescription drugs that have become a national obsession in America and now clutter the airways.

"Don't let your allergies get you down! Talk to your doctor about Claritin."

"Don't let acid indigestion stop you! It's Prilosec time."

And for those people who need a prescription fat blocker, there's Xenical. The side effects may include inability to control bowel movements, but I guess that's something you can live with if it helps you pursue the Olympic dream by getting under the weight limit in Greco-Roman wrestling or into a pair of spandex running pants.

If pseudoephedrine is performance-enhancing, so are all of the above drugs. And so are Ibuprofen, Motrin and the caffeine that's in one of the Olympics' big-time sponsors, Coca-Cola. Even Viagra is a performance-enhancing drug.

Well, the performance it enhances is still not part of the Olympics. But considering the low television ratings for the Sydney Games, I bet NBC is pushing for it to be adopted as a sport in 2004.

In the meantime, somebody should steal a gold medal and give it to the Romanian gymnast. She worked four years to earn a gold, and then had it stolen away by fine print.

Pseudoephedrine won her the gold?

As I finish my personal trial run with pseudoephedrine, I can tell you that's certainly not the case. It hasn't even helped me turn a catchy phrase or drop a silky metaphor.

But tomorrow I'll add Vicks Formula 44, some VapoRub and Chloraseptic. With that kind of enhanced performance, I'm sure I have a Pulitzer in the bag.

# A Y2K bug without any bite

We're still here! We're still here! Thank God, we're still here!

Actually, I never doubted that the size-13 sneakers of human ingenuity would squish that creepy little Y2K bug. That's why I made sure to keep the receipt for the electric generator, 150 bottles of water and half dozen shotguns I purchased last week.

Yes, our way of life appears intact early in the new millennium. After all the worrying and all the hype, we can now take comfort in knowing that the world's computers still safely store all the information of our lives, including records that indicate my Mastercard bill is overdue.

Stupid Y2K bug. I knew I couldn't count on you.

The birth of the year 2000 was a little anticlimactic, really. When it was finally America's turn to flip the zeroes, the Y2K bug was already a bigger bomb than *Ishtar* and the only panicked rioting was over portable toilets in Times Square. The world was never reduced to a smoking pile of rubble, and much more surprising, neither was ABC News anchor Peter Jennings.

Jennings' 24-hour on-air marathon provided the only exciting countdown of New Year's Eve, as we all wondered when sleep deprivation would send him into a babbling soliloquy about the state of mankind and his forbidden love for Barbara Walters. You could tell Jennings was barely hanging on in the final hours, and it seemed, barely able to stand up. But in the end, I think his on-air marathon was worth it. I certainly felt reassured that, even if all hell broke loose in the world and I didn't know if I would live another day, I could turn to ABC News to see a respected newsman pop No-Doz.

The Y2K bug's lack of bite was disappointing to some, and not just for people with closets full of camouflage. It was also a bummer for the media, which is now stuck in a Y2K news void. The only Y2K-glitch stories available are about how people are still writing 1999 on their checks, and that just doesn't compare to the drama of newspaper headlines like:

**WORLD ENDS!**
(Over $25 in coupons inside)

I admit that I'm a little disappointed that the Y2K bug was so harmless. I'm glad we're all safe, but I was hoping that, at the very least, Bob Dole's commercials for erectile dysfunction wouldn't be Y2K compliant. I also hoped that the Y2K bug would shut down all the annoying whining about how, technically, this is not the start of a new millennium.

But there was nothing, nothing at all. It turns out this is just like any other year, which was confirmed when my annual New Year's resolution didn't make it past the first week. This year's resolution to — eat healthier — ended after two days and two dinners of chocolate chip cookies and cheese popcorn.

Of course, I could just blame the Y2K bug for the dissolution of my resolution. After all, the technological gurus say that the Y2K bug could give us problems all year long. But to blame the Y2K bug would be to refuse responsibility for my own undoing. And that's something the world can't do if it wants to make it to Y3K, or at least, Y2.05K.

But can this world make it to Y3K?

Well, it's up to us. And with the new millennium upon us, this is the perfect time to evaluate our lives. This is the perfect time to decide how we're going to give back to this world from which we've taken so much. This is the perfect time to look deep inside our souls, celebrate the brotherhood of humanity, address the needs of the people of this world, and join together to pay my MasterCard bill.

# A double visionary from the very start

The keys to clear vision sure have changed over the years. Glasses and contact lenses are still around, but now there are LASIK procedures, Photo Refractive Keratectomy and other eye surgeries with more letters than an entire eye chart.

Twenty-five years ago, the keys to clear vision were much more simple: Scotch tape, masking tape, electrical tape, and occasionally, a strong piece of string.

Those were the keys for me, anyway. I wore glasses throughout my childhood, and they were usually held together in some highly unfashionable way. That's because of the childhood law, well-known by those who wear glasses, that the kid with glasses always gets hit in the face with a ball.

Flying baseballs, basketballs, footballs and soccer balls gravitated toward my face. Frisbees and wildly swung Wiffle-Ball bats also foiled many a pair of untarnished glasses. One minute I would be enjoying recess, and then wham! — I was spending 10 minutes searching for a missing lens, a broken earpiece or asking the teacher for some duct tape. Yes, duct tape. There cannot possibly be a tape more hideously unfashionable than the silvery, metallic look of duct tape, but many times it held my glasses together.

And I couldn't go without my glasses. I began wearing them when I was just 2 years old after my parents noticed a serious problem: my eyes made me look like a demonic toddler trying to hypnotize something.

I was cross-eyed. There was a more scientific word for it, but what it meant to me was that I had double vision, and more important, that I would be wearing glasses for a long time. I would wear them for my primary-school years (The "Four Eyes! Four Eyes!" Era), through junior high (The "How did you lose your glasses this time?"

Era) and for the start of high school (The "Boys who wear glasses don't make passes at girls" Era).

I hated growing up with glasses. I hated the way wearing them made me feel like a nerd, even if I really was one. I hated blindly wandering around the house trying to remember where I took them off before I went to bed. I hated the way they fogged up when I played sports, and that when it rained, my classmates would say, "Hey, you need windshield wipers!"

Then came the inevitable flying object to the face. I mention it again because flying object versus spectacles happened with amazing regularity. And the result was always the same. I would stand there with a stunned look on my face — my eyes dazed and glasses crooked in what seemed to be a parody of Woody Allen caught in a windstorm. Then I would try to readjust the glasses. It was an almost impossible task, because glasses never fit quite right after they take a direct hit from any sports equipment not created by Nerf.

Eventually, however, I didn't need to wear glasses. I was 14 when my optometrist told me that my "wandering" eye had strengthened, and I could take off my glasses for good. I did, almost expecting a soccer ball to come flying through the office to tag me one last time.

But what about the good memories of wearing glasses?

That's a question my mom would ask, because as a typical mom, she tries to put an upbeat spin on everything. She even kept many pairs of my glasses as keepsakes. Well, either as keepsakes or for spare parts.

A few months ago, she sent me the first pair of glasses I wore, apparently trying to unlock some positive memories of my glasses-wearing experience.

"Remember when you wore these?" she wrote.

Actually, I don't remember the time when I wore the tiny, black, horned-rim glasses. But I'll take her word for it. They are, after all, broken.

# Beauty of cell phones doesn't ring true

A judge in Texas is so tired of cellular phones ringing in his courtroom that he is ruling people in contempt of court for inappropriate ringing. The offending parties must pay a $100 fine or be thrown in jail.

Now that's a pretty outrageous case of a judge misusing his power. And it just steams me to think that my tax dollars are paying the salary of a judge who doesn't have the guts to make the right decision and have the cellular-phone people executed by firing squad.

I'm kidding, of course. That would be inhumane. It should be done by lethal injection.

Now before everybody starts calling me on their cellular phones and screaming, "You (static) what you're talking (static) you (static) buffoon, cell phones (static) greatest breakthrough in communica (static) history," I ask that you exit the tunnel. You sound like a stutterer with emphysema.

The truth is, I don't really have a problem with cellular phones. In fact, my wife has one in her car. But that's just for emergencies, like when we're at a red light, and I roll down my window, look over at the driver next to me and pretend I'm the phone-a-friend on *Who Wants to be a Millionaire*.

"Yes, Bob, it's definitely C — Deoxyribonucleic acid. Can I talk to Regis again?"

So there's nothing really wrong with cellular phones. But there is something very wrong with calling home from the grocery store to seek help on a mind-bending decision like whether to buy Fruity Pebbles or Cocoa Puffs. This is a perfect example of how cellular phones have taken over our lives and taken away our brains.

Can't we just think for ourselves? Can't we make such an

insignificant decision without picking up a phone? Can't we all finally realize that Cocoa Puffs are much better than Fruity Pebbles?

Apparently, the answer to all of these questions is no. It's also apparent that many people treat the ringing of their cell phone like the 11th commandment. They may let their answering machines pick up calls at home, but the cellular ring is the like the word of God. Cell-phoners pick up no matter where they are — at the movies, at their child's school play or at a funeral.

"John was a wonderful man, I don't know how I'll go on without ... hold on, I have to take this call."

But the biggest problem with cellular phones, the new digital PCS phones and the cutting-edge wireless phones with Internet and mind-control service built right in, is how dangerous it makes driving. Just this week I was cut off by a man talking on his cell phone while he was driving his Chevy Suburban, and it scared me to death. I barely had enough time to finish tuning the radio, put down my hairbrush and mirror, and swerve to avoid the irresponsible driver. I even spilled my Big Gulp.

Of course, not everyone agrees that driving while talking on a cellular phone is dangerous. And being a responsible journalist, I need to present both sides of this issue. That's why I called a spokesman for the cellular phone industry, who agreed to talk to me while he was driving.

"The idea that drivers using mobile phones are more dangerous than other drivers is just plain ridiculous," he said. "In fact, people who talk on mobile phones are AAAARGH!..."

Don't worry, he wasn't seriously injured in the accident. As for the girl scout and the little old lady who were in the crosswalk, we'll just have to keep our fingers crossed.

# Win or luge, a medal isn't worth your skeleton

If you've seen the winter Olympics, I bet you've seen the luge. That's the event where a world-class athlete puts on a Catwoman outfit, lies on his or her back, and races on a tiny sled down an icy track toward gold-medal glory and/or an untimely death.

OK, so I'm exaggerating a bit — they're not really world-class athletes. But the lugers do go like 80 mph down the track with nothing to protect them but an aerodynamic helmet and a Jacque Cousteau bodysuit. That brings up an obvious question:

In a time where great minds of the world can work together to lose an entire Mars space probe, shouldn't we be able to come together as a global community and make the luge more dangerous?

The answer, of course, is yes. That's why today, in the grand tradition of do-it-yourself dentistry and virtually every Burt Reynolds movie, I can introduce you to the newest Olympic sport, the skeleton.

The skeleton is just like the luge, only totally insane. Instead of lying on your back and going feet first, the skeleton features world-class athletes (another little joke there) lying on their stomachs racing head-first on a tiny sled toward gold-medal glory and/or an untimely death. Much like the luge, skeleton competitors must steer smoothly around the course, point their toes, and most important, find an aerodynamic way to scream in terror.

This sport may sound stupid to you, but it really isn't, at least when compared to the biathlon. The biathlon is the Olympic sport where competitors cross-country ski for a while, then pull out their rifles and take aim at targets, and hopefully, not each other. The biathlon was added to the Olympics over other equally deserving sports like basket-soccer, foot-tennis, Tae-Bo and synchronized yachting.

The biggest problem with the skeleton is finding competitors. After all, the sport will debut in 2002 at Salt Lake City — a place where it's difficult to buy alcohol — and most people need at least a six-pack before agreeing to zoom to their doom. I think Olympic organizers will need to have *The Price is Right*'s Bob Barker near the luge track yelling, "Come on down!" to get enough competitors. Then, as some poor sap is daydreaming about what kind of car he's going to win, he'll be shoved down the track toward gold- medal glory and/or an untimely death.

But hey, what do I know? I'm not an Olympic expert. All I know is that to win the gold, no matter what the sport, you *must* stick the landing. One wobbly step has shattered golden dreams for the top figure skaters, gymnasts and curlers.

Still, I wish Olympic organizers — when they weren't taking bribes — would have steered the Games away from sports' new extreme theme. I mean, if we really want to be extreme, why don't we just blindfold lugers, spin them around 10 times and then send them down the track? That would certainly determine who is an Olympic-quality athlete. Or maybe we could drop people out of airplanes and time how long it takes them to reach the ground.

"Look at how he raises his arms and makes himself like a knife to cut through the wind! That's why he is — SPLAT! — er, was, a world-class athlete."

The skeleton should have a slightly better survival rate. And it does offer you, the reader who has made it more than three-fourths of the way through this column, a chance to win an Olympic medal. Right now you are guaranteed a silver, because only one person is entered — a man from Norway who has already downed a couple of six-packs.

So step forward and take the challenge. You may be a world-class athlete and not know it. You may be the next face on a Wheaties box.

And if you lose control of your sled, fly off the track and land on your head, just remember to stick the landing.

# New hobby doth filleth my time

I spent a good part of last night sitting on my porch, staring at the starry sky and pondering just how insignificant we all are in this universe. And as I peered into the beautiful black beyond, felt the breeze on my face and watched the wispy clouds stretch across the moon, I had a revelation:

I need a hobby.

After all, I had spent an hour staring at nothing. My neighbors probably think I'm some goofball waiting for the mother ship to come and take me away.

So after hours of struggle, I've finally come up with a hobby. And with all due respect to the other outstanding hobbies like stamp collecting, needlepoint and experimenting with explosives, I believe my choice is the best.

I've become an ordained minister.

Really.

I know some of you are scoffers. You'll probably point out that I sometimes use foul language, have occasionally bent the truth and once beared false witness against my neighbor when asked who hit the baseball through the window.

My answer to that is simple: God doesn't like tattletales.

And by the way, you critics of my spiritual determination, I have a very solid religious background. I was raised a Roman Catholic, and my family went to church every week. I can even remember many of the pastor's sermons, like this one story where a man gave his two sons the same amount of money, and the sons left home and spent the money differently, and when they came home, a huge spider was chasing me and I jumped off a cliff and was flying over an ocean with an umbrella and ...

I guess I dozed off during that one.

It's not like I was the only one sliding into dreamland in church. It seemed everyone was doing the "slow melt." First the eyes would close, then the head would tilt downward, then just as the person was about to fall forward, the head would jerk back up to show the person's expression of "What the heck just happened?"

Note the use of "heck" in the previous sentence. It would've been very easy to use H-E-double-hockey-sticks for that one. Do you still question how committed I am to ministry?

Some of you probably do. Well, then I should mention that I also took a very active role in my church as a teenager. I even went on a three-day retreat for teens, where many of us learned about the presence of God in our lives and many more learned about the presence of a 24-pack of Budweiser in a suitcase. I also remember a BB gun being fired in the middle of the night, which wasn't exactly the religious awakening the instructors had promised.

But now I'm having my true religious awakening. I'm an ordained minister of the Universal Life Church, which believes in the "right to freedom of religion and to do that which is right." To be honest, I don't know much about the church, except that its tenets are as vague as the paranormal anthropology class I took in college, where as part of the final, my aura was analyzed.

The only thing that really matters is that the church allowed me to become an ordained minister over the Internet. Rev. Matt was ordained in just a couple of minutes, along with Rev. Casper, also known as my dog.

Now I'm taking my message to the people. And because I'm not one of those crazy fire-and-brimstone preachers, who like to swing Bibles while they describe how "the locusts dideth eateth out the sinners eyes," my message is simple. I just want everyone to promote kindness, respect all living things, do unto others as they would have done to them, and of course, remember that "Zeeblert" is the password for the mother ship.

# Drink up from the King of columns

Welcome to the Budweiser Matt Wixon column. For all you do, this column's for you.

Now don't panic. This is still the same important column you've relied on for years for political analysis, unbiased commentary and baking tips. It's just that financial difficulties have forced me to take on a sponsor, and thankfully, Budweiser was available.

I feel comfortable with Budweiser as my sponsor because the King of Beers understands my artistic integrity. Bud knows that, even if it is an official sponsor of my column, I am not going to waste precious space writing about how it is the finest beer on the market and has a fantastic born-on dating system. Budweiser would also never expect me to mention how it brews its beer with only the finest barley malt, rice, hops, yeast and water, or how it's now featuring limited edition millennium bottles and cans.

I also see no reason to mention Frank and Louie, the two lizards from the Budweiser commercials. They certainly have no place in this column, even if they are very cute and are reason enough for us all to enjoy an ice cold Bud.

That being said, I hope everyone understands that I am not selling out. And hey, my one sponsor is not nearly as bad as college football bowl games, which are assured of being sell-outs without selling a ticket. They're so loaded with sponsors that the announcers can't get the name out in one breath:

"Welcome to the Nabisco-Fisher Price-Poulan Weedeater-Kentucky Fried Chicken-Kellogg's Frosted Flakes Cereal Bowl presented by Black and Decker, Wells Fargo and ..."

"My God! Brent Musberger just passed out!"

The Budweiser Matt Wixon column, presented by Frito-Lay, will never be so blatantly commercial. After all, I've worked too hard to make this column what it is — something readers can turn to with confidence, knowing each week that they will get, well, about 650 words. And I must be true to my craft, just like Budweiser has been true to its craft since 1876.

That's why I am very careful when I consider adding sponsors. I tell the companies up front that I will not compromise my column just to mention, for example, that "Pizza Hut is makin' it great." I think that would be like standing up at a presidential debate and asking Al Gore, "Did somebody say McDonald's?"

In other words, goodbye credibility. And that's something I always want the Budweiser Matt Wixon column, presented by Frito-Lay and Tampax, to have. I want the column to be done my way, even if its with the help of Hanes Her Way. And when people read my column, I want them to know that they are in good hands, like with Allstate.

So while the name of the column has changed a little, my journalistic integrity certainly has not. Unfortunately, however, I'm just about out of space for this week, so I won't have room for my view of the political climate in Ghana.

But I'm glad I had this chance to let you know where I stand. For although the name may have changed a bit, the Budweiser Matt Wixon column, presented by Frito-Lay, Tampax and Viagra, will still rise above commercial influence.

And next week it will be back to business as usual, with me tackling the tough questions like, "How will global warming affect the planet?" "Will we ever achieve world peace?" and "Have you driven a Ford lately?"

# At long last, I've found paradise

Some people swear they will never live in a big city. Sure there's lots to do, but the traffic is a pain and breathing the polluted air is like sucking on a tailpipe. For others, a small town equals misery. They simply can't be happy without a Starbucks, Olive Garden and Nordstrom's to enrich their lives.

I've given it a lot of thought, too. But after weighing all the good and bad, I've decided I don't want to live in a big city or a small town. I don't want to live in the mountains, desert or by the beach, either. I want to live in a commercial.

I want to live where all the people are beautiful, all the people are delightful, and all the people talk casually about adult diapers. I want to live in an exciting place — a place where a Certs encounter can happen at any time and I can rely on my deodorant and toothpaste for 24-hour protection.

I want to live in a community of loving neighbors who I can entice into a dancing frenzy by simply popping open a can of Pringles. I want my neighbors to take the pain reliever hospitals use most and the coughing, aching, sneezing, stuffy head so-they-can-rest medicine.

I don't want my neighbors to be groggy, after all. I want them to have such a zest for life that they are willing to jump from an airplane for a diet soda, and such a passion for cleaning that they invite me over to smell their toilet. I want to live where the people never have morning breath and they chew the gum dentists recommend to their patients who chew gum.

Family is important, so I want to live where I can find a cereal my whole family can enjoy. At dinner, I want us to come together around a steaming bowl of soup, especially if it's the soup that eats like a meal. And later in the evening, I want to be able to talk longer with distant family members in the security of knowing I dialed 10-10-321, or better yet, dialed 1-800-COLLECT and charged the call to them.

I want to live in a world where there's an easy cure for wrinkles on my face and wrinkles in my clothes. I want my children to walk to school feeling downy fresh, and in colors that are bright and whites that are white. When they come home, I want to solve their problems with a bottle of Sunny Delight.

I want to live in a place where I can find success with healthy-looking hair, and I can do it without the hassle of shampooing and conditioning. I want to live where a pill will reverse my increasing waistline and receding hairline, and where I can blend away my gray so naturally that nobody knows my secret.

I want to live where everything is new and improved, value-sized and packaged for my convenience. I want to scramble an egg in its shell, clap on and clap off and clean my floors with a space-age polymer that's imported from Sweden.

I want a product that will change my life and I want to pay for it in three easy payments.

I want to live where I can expect more from my truck, obey my thirst and make more money by studying at home for my degree in TV/VCR repair. I want to chat with my smiling entrepreneurial neighbor with the big plastic head, do the Chow Chow Chow with my cat and have a dog who speaks Spanish when he's craving Mexican food.

Most important, I want to live where I'm respected. I want the credit I deserve, a low fixed interest rate for the first six months and no payments until the year 2003. And I definitely want my satisfaction to be guaranteed.

I hope someday I'll find this place, where the scrubbing bubbles work hard so I don't have to, and I can soften hands while I do dishes. My heart burns for such a utopia.

Good thing I took some Pepto Bismol.

# Buy low, sell high and always keep the beat

The New York Stock Exchange is a lot like MTV's Spring Break party. Just bear with me a minute here, OK?

The music may be a little different on the ticker-tape floor and clothing isn't optional away from the beach, but both places have a lot of trading going on. In New York it's stocks, while on the beach it's phone numbers, nose rings and embarrassing conditions that require a trip to the doctor. And when the final bell rings and the last deejay packs up, everybody rocks the house with claps and cheers.

What a party!

That's why I had to get in on it. The stock market party, anyway.

Of course I couldn't just waltz down to the NYSE and start trading. They don't just let anyone in there, which is probably a good thing, because I don't know any of the hand signals and might call someone a nerd while trying to purchase shares of Nerf.

I also know almost nothing about investing. But I do know that the stock market keeps going up, and that if I don't start saving early, I may be spending my 70th birthday as the fry guy at McDonald's. So I picked a wise-looking financial adviser and asked for some help.

"First of all, we need to determine your tolerance for risk," my adviser said. "Just how much fluctuality can you handle in the value of your stock portfolio?"

"Well," I said, "I don't want to lose any money."

"Yes, but how aggressive do you want to be in your investing?" he said.

"Well," I said, "I don't want to lose any money."

Apparently I just wasn't getting it, because he looked at me like I had mutual funds crawling out of my ears. And he said my plan to put away five bucks a month so I could retire at age 35 was not realistic, even if I was diligent about cutting back on vending-machine Twinkies.

He was just like the handful of financial gurus and world-full of financial-guru wannabes that I have spoken to. He advised me to invest in growth stocks, which often increase in value rapidly but sometimes drop out of sight faster than Tickle Me Elmo. It was important to be aggressive, he said, adding that "historically, the stock market is the best place to put your money."

Yes, but historically, there was The Great Depression. And historically, after working 40 years to save for retirement, many people find it more than a little distressing to beg for loose change.

Needless to say, I won't be appearing in a Merrill Lynch ad anytime soon. I'm a breed apart from the people who can happily say that a 3,000-point market drop won't bother them. I also get a little concerned about the fine print on the bottom of my investment prospectus:

"Results may vary. You may gain or lose money. And please remember, even if a market crash turns your portfolio into a port-fail-io, it is illegal in most countries to shoot your fund manager."

It was scary, but I finally gave in. In the hopes of one day being part of the Generation of Commas and Lots of Zeroes, I put my MTV Generation money on the line. I can't remember exactly what I invested in, but I believe it was 10 percent in technology stocks, 10 percent in blue-chip stocks and 80 percent in some beautiful swamp land in Louisiana.

I've never actually seen the land, but the brochure assures me that it's beautiful.

# Welcome! Press 1 for a long wait

It's a well-known fact that we sleep away a third of our lives, give or take a couple presses of the snooze bar. That's an easy one to figure out — we average about eight hours of sleep per day, whether it's in a bed, on a couch or in front of a computer at work.

But other mesmerizing minutiae of our lives isn't so easy to break down. That's why we need teams of well-trained and well-paid researchers to come up with the rest of the mind-blowing statistical data.

According to their research, we spend years of our lives in the bathroom and months standing in lines. We even spend weeks of our lives brushing our teeth, and that doesn't include a flossing regimen that would make our dentists proud.

Ah, so that's why we're always running behind. No wonder there's never enough time for you and I to do all the things we want and for the Reverend Jerry Falwell to condemn them. This pie of life baked up by the reality-based researchers has way too many pieces.

And another huge piece of this sad pie, a piece we all eventually get to deal with, isn't even accounted for — holding for the next available representative.

"Thank you for calling customer service. We value your call. All of our operators are busy helping customers right now. The approximate wait time is 10 minutes."

Their estimate redefines the word "approximate." They must not know that several of the service reps are seeing movies on their lunch breaks or that one customer is attempting to take over the company while his call is monitored for quality assurance.

"Thank you for pressing the number 3. Press the number 3 again for more options on what numbers to press. Press the number 4 if you would like to be told to press letters instead of numbers. Thank you for waiting for these last 15 minutes. You're approximate wait time is 10 minutes."

After 15 minutes I'm still waiting and whistling along with the hold music. Thirty minutes later, I wish I had pressed 2 for Spanish so I could at least learn a new language while I approached deficit-spending on my time budget.

An hour later, I'm still waiting, cursing the orchestral version of "Stairway to Heaven," and feeling trapped by the threat that I'll lose my place.

"Don't hang up, as we respond to the calls in the order that they are received."

That's the kicker. If I hang up, I'll get punted to the back of the line behind the other poor saps in telephonic torture. So I'm not going anywhere, even if I may be reported as a missing person. I just wish my pre-recorded friend would tell me the truth.

"Thank you for calling customer service. Steve, Mary and Joe quit about 45 minutes ago and the rest of us are still being trained. You're approximate wait time is ... well, you might want to get a sandwich or something. Do you have any reading material?

Yes, customer service really is a big pain in the neck. And a big piece of the pie. So I called up the researchers and asked why they left the customer service numbers out of the equation.

I mean, how could these trained professionals gloss over such critical information? I'll tell you their answer later. They put me on hold.

# Video didn't kill all the radio stars

No matter what anybody says, Mister Microphone was a quality item.

Sure, the seventies gizmo from the creators of life-changing products like the Pocket Fisherman and the Breathe-Free Smokeless Ashtray had some glitches. Sometimes it was easier to tune in Manitoba or an orbiting satellite than your own voice on the radio, and other times Mister Microphone just plain wouldn't work.

But when it worked, it was magical. You would turn on Mister Mike, dial your radio to the correct frequency, and ... "Hey babe, I'll be back to pick you up later!"

Well I tried, but it was hard to be as groovy as those hipsters in the Mister Microphone commercial. I lacked a car, didn't have an afro or lambchop sideburns, and "babes" weren't too attracted to a 7-year-old in Toughskins. But with my Mr. Microphone I could really belt out Jim Croce's "Bad, Bad Leroy Brown" — much to the chagrin of my family and neighbors.

I really did like hearing my voice on that radio, even if I was more out of tune than the Mr. Microphone. And I guess I'm not alone. People obviously enjoy hearing their voice on the air, because that can be the only explanation for the amazing popularity of radio talk shows.

They are certainly not the forum for public commentary the hosts probably envisioned. Radio talk shows are more like a telephone party line, where few people know who they're talking to and even less know what they're talking about.

We've all been in on the party. We've all called in at some point in our lives, whether it was to make a valid comment, tell the host off or just say something crude and see if it could survive the seven-second delay.

The shows can also be addicting. When I was growing up, I was so hooked on getting my voice on the air that I would call the fishing show every night. The only thing I knew about fish was that tuna was three-for-a-dollar at Safeway, but I just couldn't get through on any of the other shows.

Not that the topic matters on talk radio, anyway. Listeners regard the day's topic as a mere suggestion.

**Host:** Hello, you're on the "Holy Cow: That's Me on the Radio!" show. Today's topic is teen pregnancy. What's on your mind, caller?

**Caller:** Yes, hello. Oh my gosh, I think I'm on the air. Can you hold on a minute? Honey, start taping, I'm on the air! (high-pitched squeal in the background)

**Host:** Yes, you're on the air. Please turn down your radio so I can hear you.

**Caller:** Oh, I'm sorry. I'm a long-time listener but a first-time caller. I really love your show. I listen to the show all the time on the way to work, and even sometimes at work, although my boss gets real cranky when I listen to the radio or play around on the Internet. I really like the Internet. But there's a lot of that adult stuff on the Internet, too. I think we need to do something about that.

**Host:** Uh, do you have a comment for today's topic?

**Caller:** Yes I do. What was the topic again?

**Host:** Teen pregnancy.

**Caller:** Oh that's right. Teen pregnancy is very sad. I also think guns are bad, but only when they hurt people, kind of like President Clinton, when he looked us all in the face and lied. That bas...

**Host:** OK, let's move on.

That's exactly what I've decided to do. No matter how

entertaining the shows may be, I'm quitting my talk-radio habit cold turkey. There must be a better way to spend my time.

Especially if I can find that Mr. Microphone.

# Don't cry, or tape over, spilled milk

OK, parents. I know your child is adorable, lovable and an absolute darling who makes the Gerber baby look like a castoff from the Planet Ugly. You can put away the photos now.

I also know it's natural to feel you must preserve your precious memories. What a shame it would be to forget the way your bundle of joy smiles, cries or calls the Chili's waiter ugly.

And don't children say the darndest things?

Well, I'll have to take your word on that one, because I don't have any kids yet. But I do know that parents say the darndest things, and those darn things get darn embarrassing when they are on tape.

My parents learned that the hard way. One night they decided to secretly tape the family dinner, probably figuring that 10 years later listening to the conversation of their little dears would be a real hoot.

And most of our "suppers" were pretty amusing back then. My 3-year-old brother was a stutterer and needed a whole meal to get out "Please pass the peas." (Note: I know that stuttering can be a serious problem, but I can joke about my brother because he no longer stutters. Plus, I'm bigger than him.)

Apparently the tape was extremely secret. It was so secret, in fact, that my parents forgot to stay in Ward and June Cleaver mode for the whole dinner.

Even worse, they forgot to erase the tape.

And a decade later, as a nerdy teenager looking for a blank tape to record some new Michael Jackson song off the radio, I found it.

Jackpot. Suddenly the precocious child of 1975 was considering ferocious blackmail in 1985. And it wasn't because I finally realized why I couldn't get those dang Freddy Fender tunes out of my head.

I knew I had something special when I heard — over the backdrop of Freddy's "Before the Last Teardrop Falls" — unidentifiable children talking and then my mom's very identifiable voice yelling, "Shut up!" Of course, her kids didn't shut up. We never shut up.

But the real star of the evening was my dad. And before I reveal the contents of my version of the Zapruder tape, I must say that my dad is one of the nicest people I know and that I feel blessed to have him as my role model.

But not on that day in 1975. I think dear ol' dad was a little on edge, and he went over the edge when I spilled my glass of milk. The result was an audio disaster worse than a Britney Spears album:

"What happened?" my mom asked. "Oh, Matt just spilled his whole damn glass of milk!" my dad yelled.

He then added, "Well, if he can't drink his milk the right way, he can just sit in it."

And sit in it, I did. All the way through Freddy Fender's greatest hits. But years later, I was able to make enough copies of the tape for everyone in the family and get my dad to pay for my entire college education.

Seriously, I thought it was pretty funny 10 years after my dinner in the milk puddle. But others in my position might not. They may need to seek therapy, throw a guilt trip on their parents or write a column about it.

So be careful, parents. The roles may someday be reversed. You may need your children to take care of you — bathe you, wash your clothes and fix you a nice meal complete with a tall glass of milk.

In that case, I suggest you don't spill the whole damn glass.

# Candy-coated crime does pay off at the movies

Movie theatres should stop worrying about installing bigger screens, digital sound and luxury seats to boost their profits. They should also forget about trying to stop theatre-switchers and the people trying to sneak in the exit doors.

If the theatres really want to make the big bucks, the solution is simple: put some muscle behind "No outside food or drink allowed in the theatres."

The rule, which is broken more often than the hand dryers in movie theatre bathrooms, is usually posted by the ticket window. I guess that way people can snicker at the rule as they enter the theatre with their Snickers.

Wake up theatres, the honor code isn't working. Maybe you need a bouncer who is willing to frisk moviegoers for their secret Skittles, cloaked Clark or hidden Heath bar. Or maybe you need X-ray machines at the front doors. That's the only you can stop the snack smugglers and their scam's most ingenious weapon: the big purse.

I know of the big purse because I am a reformed — well, somewhat reformed — snack smuggler. I grew up in a family where our movie treats were usually whatever contraband we could cram into my mom's purse.

A lot fits in a purse, too. Take out the lipstick, Kleenex, make-up mirrors and checkbook and there is plenty of room for a half dozen candy bars and a six-pack of sodas.

Well, at least my mom's purse had that much room. Of course, it wasn't her everyday purse. The "movie purse," which was a little like a fashionable grocery bag, was a specialized tool to stretch our family's movie dollar.

I can't exactly blame my parents for involving their children in such a sinister plot. Kids at a concession stand usually want everything, including the drink that's bigger than their bladder. And the prices of soda, popcorn and candy at the movies are reminiscent of the old *Wheel of Fortune* format, where contestants had to spend $250 of their winnings on a deluxe toaster or ceramic duck.

In fact, the first time I was old enough to go to the movies by myself, I brought only two dollars for candy and soda. I was too young to know that a theatre is a little world of its own, where the prices are set by the same people selling the government $100 toilet seats. It turned out that, although I was finally grown up enough to go solo at the Harkins, I only had enough money for the "child" size drink.

Even in today's money, you'd think three dollars would get me some very special M&Ms in my movie pack. But they're the same ol' M&Ms from down at the drug store, just marked up more than a loaf of bread in Russia.

That's why before every movie, my parents would take us over to the store to stock up on the tastiest promoters of tooth decay. Sometimes we'd even bring popcorn from home, which was neatly divided and wrapped in sandwich bags.

Cheap? Well, maybe. But prepared, yes.

The only problem was finding the right time to pop the top on our sodas. You needed a nice loud point in the movie to avoid suspicion. And if you let the aluminum can roll down the theatre floor, you could bet the theatre's junior detective would be shining his flashlight down your row.

This snack smuggling may seem a little ridiculous, but I know there are others who grew up in a cinematic crime family like mine. After all, we all love a good deal. That's why a 98-cent store recently opened in my neighborhood and undercut the obviously overpriced 99-cent store.

But as I said, I'm reformed. I would never do that kind of thing again.

I let my wife carry the purse.

# Stop crying, you'll love summer camp

The parent-child bond is rarely stronger than when the summer-camp bus pulls out of the parking lot. Children press their faces against the windows and flash teary eyes that ask, "How can you do this to me?"

Let's see, where should parents start? There's the fruit-punch stain on the carpet and the broken window in the living room. There's the T-shirt that got flushed down the toilet and the dent in the wall from a game of indoor baseball. And can somebody please explain how a chair from the kitchen table ended up in the pool?

Yes, parents have their reasons to pack the kids off to Camp Idontwannago.

But camp is supposed to be fun, not punishment. So when departure day arrives, and some kids act like it's more punishment than privilege, parents naturally worry.

They worry that their child will get lonely. They worry that their child will get lost. They worry that their child will get lonely, then lost, then bitten by a snake coiled in Poison Ivy in a flash-flood area near a dangerous ledge.

Relax, parents. Your children are having a great time. They are riding horses, telling stories around the campfire and learning how to steer canoes. That or a search party will soon find them.

I'm kidding, of course. As a camp counselor during my teenage years, I don't recall ever losing a camper. We lost at least one sock each day, a pair of shoes per week, and over the course of the summer, several comic books and a couple of asthma inhalers. But we never lost a whole person — unless you count counselors, who sometimes discovered midway through camp that they must have lost their minds to accept such a job.

For kids, however, camp is usually fantastic. Whether they go to a sports camp, fine-arts camp, computer camp or wilderness camp, they make new friends and memories that last a lifetime. My wife, for example, went to a gymnastics camp and will never forget when a fellow camper hit her on the head with a flashlight during a fight over who would sleep on the top bunk. She also got sick on the last day, took medicine that turned her tongue black and thought she was dying. But other than that, she reports that camp was a good experience.

She also learned a lot, which is an integral part of every camp. Summer campers learn independence (no parents to cling to), bravery (trying to find the bathroom at night) and ingenuity (how to lather up some fun by puncturing a shaving-cream bottle with a needle and throwing it into another cabin). These are important skills each camper will use in the future, or at least in his or her first week of college.

Unfortunately, some camps are very expensive, which makes it hard on parents. Prices in the thousands are not unusual, and camps don't ease the burden by including "FREE CAMP T-SHIRT PROVIDED" in their pamphlets. For $3,000, a free T-shirt better not be the highlight of camp. I would think each camper would get several T-shirts, some shorts and an extra pair of shoes, which would come in handy. Shoes just seem to disappear during camp — and don't ask me how — are found stuck in high branches of trees.

The price is something to consider, but parents should remember that summer camp memories are priceless for kids. And when camp ends, and your child comes running to you, with one shoe missing and no sock on the other foot, calling your name and proudly waving a ceramic ashtray made especially for you, is there anything more priceless than that?

How about this: A few weeks of not hauling anyone to the movies or discovering a kitchen chair floating in the pool.

# The king of everything Irish

Another St. Patrick's Day has crept up on me, leaving me no time to shop for St. Patrick's Day presents, send out St. Patrick's Day cards, decorate the house with green lights and go St. Patrick's Day caroling.

It's probably a good thing. I bet the house with a huge, glowing shamrock on the front door wouldn't get an invitation to the next neighborhood party.

But my grandpa would be green with envy over such a display of Irish heritage. Nobody celebrated St. Patrick's Day like Eugene McKenna, the king of everything Irish. He played Irish music. Wore a green bow tie and green derby hat. Even had green mashed potatoes for dinner. I think he longed for a time when his favorite holiday would become so big that newspapers would have headlines like "Retailers hope sales slump will end with St. Patrick's Day rush."

His Irish fervor only trickled down to me. St. Patrick's Day meant mint shamrock candies and green lollipops, but in my childhood world, it couldn't compare with the gluttonous joy of a Christmas or birthday. And the history of St. Patrick's Day was a mystery. For all I knew, the holiday started when St. Patrick discovered the Blarney Stone while running from a bunch of classmates who were trying to pinch him because he wasn't wearing green.

That's what St. Patrick's Day meant to a 9-year-old. To a 29-year-old, it means remembering my grandpa.

He died when I was 13, well after he had become one of my heroes. I even believe I was predestined for the newspaper business because he worked for many years at the *St. Paul Pioneer Press* in Minnesota.

He was a pressman, but I think he should have wrote stories. He could sure tell them. And he never let the facts get in the way of a good one.

He would point to the navel on his Santa Claus belly and say, "That's where I got shot in the war." He also told me that he once ran so fast that people only saw a blur. A green blur, of course.

But my grandpa's most famous story came when my friends and I were playing basketball in the driveway — on the basketball hoop he made for me.

"I once made 10 free throws in a row blindfolded," he said, grabbing our attention. "And I shot them backward."

He added that he put light bulbs around the rim during the free throws and didn't break one. He then offered to duplicate the feat when the darn charley horse in his leg went away.

Not surprising, the darn charley horse never went away. But neither did my grandpa's imprint on the family.

Each St. Patrick's Day it was obvious. My mother would put up decorations, dress us up in green clothes and plop green derby hats on our heads, at least until we were old enough to object. One year my mom even served green milk with dinner.

Irish pride aside, milk just shouldn't be green. My mom kept telling my brother, sister and me that it was just food dye, but getting that green milk to go down took more than the luck of the Irish.

Thankfully, I have the luck of the Irish. The luck of spending much of my childhood with two heroes, my dad and my grandpa. I remember my luck when I see the picture of my grandpa reclining in the La-Z-Boy, sound asleep with his mouth wide open. I'm sitting on his knee, reclining on him, sound asleep with my mouth wide open.

That's why, even if I'm only part Irish, I celebrate St. Patrick's Day. There won't be any St. Patrick's Day caroling or a green glow to the house this year, but to honor my grandpa, maybe I'll give green milk another try.

On St. Patrick's Day, I want his Irish eyes to be smiling.

# I'll be on tambourine, but who'll be on kazoo?

Music can touch a person like nothing else. That's what my elementary school music teacher loved to tell my class — right before yelling at us to put away the maracas and stop banging on the xylophone.

"And I don't want to see anybody even getting near the cow bell," she would scream.

Obviously, my third-grade class touched her in a very special way. She was so touched, in fact, that she quit in the middle of the school year. I think her breaking point was when we struggled for three weeks to learn the harmony of "Joy to the World."

For the record, I cannot be blamed for that. I was part of the tambourine section, and although I may be a little biased, I believe we were excellent. The group playing the triangles was also very good, although I remember that the harmonica section was a little shaky.

It was quite an interesting version of "Joy to the World," a version that I'm sure didn't have Three Dog Night's blessing. We also did unflattering versions of The Beatles' "Yellow Submarine" — we renamed it "Rotten Tangerine" — and Shirley Temple's "Good Ship Lollipop," which featured a moving kazoo solo.

That's what our teacher, Ms. Shankey, was working with. So I felt bad for her, especially because she tried very, very hard. I hope that she eventually found a class of musical prodigies who didn't need a full month to learn "Hot Cross Buns" on the song flute.

And she was right. Music really can touch a person like nothing else. I know hearing a song by Yanni always takes me back to the first time I heard a Yanni song and raced to the radio to change the station.

I also remember back in high school when I first heard the song that struck a chord in my soul, the song that truly taught me a lesson about the world:

*We like the cars, the cars that go boom.*
*We're Trina and Bunny, and we like the boom.*

That song was a big Eighties hit for Trina and Bunny, or whatever their names were. The song was made up of a bass beat that sounded like a small nuclear explosion, with lyrics describing how the two girls liked, well, I guess it's obvious.

What the song made obvious to me was that anyone can be a rock star. That's why I remember it so well, and that's why, after 10 years of stalling, I'm starting a band.

This may seem unrealistic, considering I don't sing, dance, play an instrument or resemble any member of the Backstreet Boys. To be honest, I have nothing going for me musically other than a compact disc player and three different aliases in a CD club.

But I do have a vision, as well as a tambourine.

Now I'm looking for several "musicians" who want to be part of the most innovative group ever. Music ability is not required, and frankly, not encouraged. A musical hotshot who has mastered "Hot Cross Buns" on the song flute might make me jealous and tear the group apart like Yoko Ono tore apart The Beatles.

That might be our only connection with the Fab Four, but I have high hopes.

Someday, we'll all be rich and famous. Someday, we'll write the songs that make the whole world sing, or at least play along with a kazoo.

Someday, our music will touch Ms. Shankey like nothing else.

# How may I help you? This is a recording

I'm not one to brag, but I know a lot about customer service. So shut up and read this column.

Just kidding. Obviously that is the wrong attitude to have when speaking with customers, unless you work as a dominatrix.

That's one of the things I learned — changing my attitude, not the dominatrix part — in a recent customer-service program where I work. The class taught me how to be a good listener, how to solve problems and something else that I missed because I was busy trying to solve my listening problem.

But I'm sure what I missed was something about being nice to customers, which truly is very important. After all, customers are the only reason a business survives. So it's important to show them due respect, courtesy and appreciation, and most important, make sure you never close five minutes before you're supposed to when they really want a fruit smoothie.

Sorry about injecting my personal experience there. I'm sure that the coffee-and-juice joint that rejected me doesn't normally turn away customers who have already walked through the door. Perhaps they were overwhelmed by two customers coming in at the same time or there was a bagel crisis behind the counter. You just never know. But in my opinion, they can take their fruit and ...

Whoa! Where did that come from? It's that dang attitude again. That attitude that I can absolutely not have if I want to excel at customer service.

And I do want to excel. But I also realize that the odds are stacked against me because I am not like most people.

Most people, at least according to the latest commercials featuring real actors in actual reenactments, hate speaking to a machine. They want to speak to an actual person who actually pretends to care.

I, on the other hand, love machine language. "Press 1 for this, Press 2 for that" is just fine with me as long as I don't have to speak to the helpful service rep who puts me on hold for an hour or accidentally connects me to the dial-tone department.

A few weeks ago, my hotel-reservations buddy zapped me into telephonic hyperspace and then accidentally booked me into two different hotels for the same night. Luckily, a machine caught the error. Thank you very much, Mr. Roboto.

That's why I think talking to a machine is the way to go. I even think machines would be a great replacement for waiters, who I find nauseatingly helpful.

I know there's a tip on the line, but I hate when waiters give me the guided tour through my meal. "How was that bite? And how about that one? Can I take your plate? Can I take your wallet?"

Maybe it's because I'm shy or just plain antisocial, but I'd also like a machine to cut my hair. Nothing against hair-care professionals, who usually go about their jobs with diligence, skill, and a frighteningly sharp pair of scissors, but I don't like to talk about my life unless I'm at a therapist. I'm almost to the point where I'm going to start making stuff up, or at least start rooting for my male pattern baldness.

I did say I was different than most, and that's why mastering customer service is an uphill battle for me. But I'm not going to give up, according to my boss. So whatever it takes to be a customer-service gem, I'm going to do it. And as of today, I pledge that I will always greet your call with professional courtesy, provide you with the best possible service and ask you if you would like to open a Dillard's charge account.

Oops, wrong job.

But give me a call and try me out. I sincerely want you to know that I care and how nice you look today. And if you don't like what you hear, you can always use the automated system.

Press 1 for an angry hang-up or press 2 for "Same to you, buddy!"

# This just in: Hurricanes are scary

Hello, I'm Rock Bottom and welcome to the late news from the Channel 7 Eyewitness Action News Station, the station where you get the real news for your real life because we care about your news and we have a camera.

Our top story: Hurricane Floyd is windy, rainy and downright dangerous. In fact, as you can see from this actual footage of trees falling down, windows breaking and people evacuating the area, you'd have to be crazy to be anywhere near Floyd.

We now go to weatherman Chuck McSunshine, who is reporting live from the scene.

**CHUCK:** This is Chuck McSunshine reporting live from Hurricane Floyd for the Channel 7 Eyewitness Action News Station, the station where you get the real news for your real life because we care about your news and we have a camera. The winds are extremely strong, the rain is getting heavier and I'm about to be swept off this pier by a 10-foot tidal wave. Now back to you guys.

**ROCK:** Hey Chuck, I bet you wish you were here in the nice warm studio. But I guess this is what you get for giving us all those hot days back in August, huh? Seriously though, that's a very dangerous storm out there, isn't it?

**CHUCK:** Yes, it really is. Power lines are being knocked down, some roads are flooded and the mayor has declared a state of emergency, although I can't tell you exactly what he said because my notes blew away with my hairpiece. I can now hear windows breaking behind me, emergency sirens blaring, and I'm having some trouble keeping my balance. Do any of you have any duct tape or strong ropes?

**ROCK:** Ha, ha, Chuck. Always joking around. Just how

extensive is the damage from this terrible, terrible storm?

**CHUCK:** Well, it's really hard to tell because my glasses blew away about an hour ago.

**ROCK:** Now that is very disturbing. This storm is really hitting home. Are there places near the storm where people who have suffered such a tragedy can get their glasses replaced?

**CHUCK:** What? I don't know. Does anybody have a life jacket I can use?

**ROCK:** So what's the mood of the people out there?

**CHUCK:** There aren't any people out here. They all left during the mandatory evacuation, and maybe I should've left with them. My life is beginning to pass before my eyes, along with several mobile homes.

Hey, wouldn't our viewers have to be morons to believe a hurricane isn't dangerous? Do they really have to watch me get tossed like a salad out here?

**ROCK:** Chuck, stay at the scene. Our studies indicate that our viewers *are* morons. That's why we do in-depth stories on child abuse in under a minute and run the same stories over and over each day. And remember, we're the Channel 7 Eyewitness Action News Station, the station where you get the real news for your real life because we care about your news and we have a camera. How will our viewers know how dangerous this hurricane is if you're not on the scene?

Chuck?

Are you there, Chuck?

# Grumpy old Ned keeps on truckin'

Getting old is inevitable, but it's hard to watch a loved one begin to show the signs of age. That's why it was so difficult for me to take Ned to the doctor for what I worried might be a crushing prognosis.

"Can he be saved?" I asked. "Will he need more tests? What about a transplant?"

Thankfully, the news was good. "He's still got a lot of miles in him," said the doctor, who I believe was named Gus.

So home I went with Ned, my trusty 7-year-old truck.

Yes, I know it's a little strange to name your truck. But spending 108,000 miles together brings a certain closeness, even to inanimate objects that have trouble starting on cold mornings.

I had hoped to bring Ned great fame in a Nissan commercial, but apparently my 100,000-mile story isn't prime-time material. I guess it's because I haven't driven up mountainsides, competed in off-road rallies or hauled a barn across the country like the guys who bleed machismo in the Nissan ads. But I have missed on-ramps and misread directions enough to unintentionally explore much of Arizona, Utah, Nevada and Texas, and let me tell you, Ned is excellent at U-turns.

I think my strong, and probably unhealthy, affection for my truck comes from my failed relationship with a Ford Tempo. It was a stormy two-year affair punctuated by monthly breakdowns, including a broken fuel pump on the freeway that left me with less horsepower than Fred Flintstone's car. And unfortunately, I didn't have the courtesy of Fred's two feet, like in *The Flintstones* theme song.

My most memorable problem, however, happened in Flagstaff, Ariz. Many residents probably remember it as the famous Midnight

Idiot Parade. That's when a pair of wires in the Tempo got crossed, and any time I turned the steering wheel right or left, the horn blared. Luckily, a friend gave me some advice on how to fix it. But that was after 100 or so people had given me something else — the finger.

That's why I love my truck. Sure, the dashboard is cracking, the bumper is rusting and the air vents sometimes sound like a ticking egg-timer. And truth be told, enough of Ned's horses have left the corral over the years to make 80 mph a challenge. These days, getting over 75 gives him a case of the shakes, but I figure that's just Ned being a wise old owl.

"Sonny, why do you have to go that dang fast? Now get me my Ben-Gay!"

He's a little cranky, but as reliable as any good grandfather. Well, that was until recently, when he began sputtering and complaining when I hit the gas pedal. And even worse, he started coughing up oil all over the place. I figured he was a goner, that the egg-timer was about to hit zero.

Actually, the repairs were pretty simple. Ned had a cracked doohickey and the crank-oil-container-shaft- mechanism needed to be rethreaded with a double-barreled piston plug-a-ma-jig. That's about as technical as I can get, even with interpretive help from my grease-stained guru, Gus.

The important thing was that Ned could be saved.

Unfortunately, there's just no respect for elderly automobiles. There was no senior citizen discount, and the new trucks in the lot next to the repair shop were rudely flaunting their shiny paint jobs and ability to go 75 mph without a hitch.

Pretty flashy, those new cars. But I'm sticking with Ned, and hopefully, he'll be sticking with me. The prognosis looks good — he's not coughing up oil, all the thing-a-ma-jigs are working well and we even made it up to 75 with no complaints yesterday.

And dare I say, Ned is U-turning like a 5-year-old again.

# Passengers, we apologize for the bulging pants

An exciting innovation in aviation history occurred recently when an airline apologized to its passengers for poor service. The apology came in a commercial, and here's the really amazing part — the airline blamed itself for the problems.

That's right. The airline strayed from the industry standard of excuse handling, which for years has been much more efficient than baggage handling:

"We at Worldwide Airlines would like to apologize for the short delay of flight 1075, which is being grounded because of severe weather in the Midwest. We would also like to apologize for the late departure of flight 1225, which is being delayed by the many passengers who did not have their picture IDs ready when asked, as well as severe weather in the Midwest. We would also like to apologize to the passengers on flight 1400 who, through no fault of our own, did not receive bananas with their lunch because of the global banana famine and severe weather in the Midwest."

Until the recent commercial opened a runway to honesty, it was never the airlines' fault. And if you complained, the attitude was basically, "Look, we took off, we landed, you didn't have to use your seat cushion as a flotation device — we at Worldwide Airlines call that a successful flight."

That's why the recent commercial was as much a breath of fresh air as the law that outlawed smoking on domestic flights. Now I'm hoping the airlines will take the apologies a step further:

"We at Worldwide Airlines would like to apologize for the short, three-hour delay of flight 1450, with service to Miami. This flight is being delayed because, in addition to severe weather in the

Midwest, we scheduled too many flights, our pilots have flown too many hours and the flight attendants are threatening to strike because they are tired of explaining the banana shortage to passengers. Maybe if we were as meticulous in management as we are in getting your seat in a locked and upright position for landing, we wouldn't be making this announcement."

Even if we don't see that announcement anytime soon, there is other good news for air passengers. Airports are beefing up security to ensure your safety as you wait for your delayed flight.

Evidence of the new focus on security came earlier this summer, when police arrested a man attempting to smuggle a dozen lizards into the United States in his underwear. It happened at an airport in Las Vegas, where police noticed a man with unusual bulges around his groin (enter your joke here). In his underwear were several tube socks stuffed with nine dead lizards and three live ones, all of them native to Southeast Asia and Africa.

Now that's security we can all appreciate.

Let's say your flight has been delayed by — give me a moment to warm up my official airlines delayed-flight excuse generator — a thunderstorm that has created high winds in the area and required several flight attendants to head home for more hair spray. The last thing you want to see is a man with lizards stuffed in his pants, even if he is just trying to impress the ladies. And imagine if those Nile monitor lizards and geckos got loose in the airport. They would be out for blood, considering I'm often a little cranky after flights, and I've never had to spend a flight stuffed in a guy's pants.

Hopefully, other would-be lizard smugglers will learn from the original lizard-crotch, who was found guilty of violating the Endangered Species Act and failing to declare the lizards. He could get up to six months in prison on his sentencing date, which is scheduled for Dec. 8 but is expected to be delayed by severe weather in the Midwest.

# Breaking out on a face near you

For years newspapers have discussed ways to attract young readers, the coveted demographic group that is energetic, influential and most important, willing to pay $15 for a Puff Daddy CD. I was in on many of the attract-the-young-reader meetings and I got a lot out of them.

For example, at a meeting a few months ago, I got cookies. Then at the last meeting, I got cookies *and* donuts. I'm still not sure how to attract young readers, but if we want to attract them to a meeting, I suggest cookies and donuts.

Getting them to read the newspaper, however, is much more difficult. That's because while newspapers like to say they are reaching out to a young audience, they still insist on running important stories on political turmoil, medical breakthroughs and how leading economic indicators show that the economy grew 0.3 percent this month. Young readers don't care about any of that, unless the improved economy means the new Screaming Sonic Death Pilots CD will now only be $11.99.

So I've decided to blaze a trail to the young readers this week by hitting on a topic that really affects them. And with proms coming up, I think this is the perfect time to squeeze in this subject, which is popping up and breaking out all over the country.

That's right, I'm talking about pimples. And I have good news, young adults of America. Pimples don't have to destroy prom night the way a girl can, by saying straight to your face, in front of everyone, that you are "too geeky" to escort her on the big night.

First of all, it's a myth that pimples are caused by eating greasy food or having a dirty face. Pimples are actually caused by a physiological process that begins when you have impure thoughts or don't properly respect your elders. According to clinical studies funded by senior-citizen associations, loud music also contributes to breakouts severe enough to render Industrial Strength Clearasil useless.

It sounds strange, but it's like totally for sure true. For reals.

But don't panic, because pimples aren't nearly as noticeable as you think. Sure, people will see them. But your true friends know that the real you is on the inside, where excess oil combines with dead skin cells, clogs pores and creates that whopper of a zit right in the middle of your forehead that not even the minds of Minolta can airbrush out of your photos.

Yuck. Has your date canceled yet? Did something SUDDENLY come up?

Sorry, I'm supposed to be helping here. So here's something for all you promgoers — a tip from celebrity makeup artist Michael Criscuolo on how to cover up pimples.

Drumroll, please.

Here is the tip: Criscuolo says mixing a bit of green concealer with your foundation will pull the redness right out of the skin.

Pretty neat, huh? You too can look like one of the pore-free models of Calvin Klein ads. Just make sure you don't use too much makeup, or you'll end up looking like Al Gore right before a debate.

Finally, if you can't conceal the pimple with makeup, covering it with a tattoo is an option. Many of the cool kids are getting tattoos anyway, and your parents won't mind if you tell them it's essential to your self-esteem.

So good luck with your big night. I hope these tips will help you leaders of tomorrow be the beautiful, handsome, formally-dressed Jack in the Box customers of today.

And now that I've taken a step to reach out to you young readers, I hope you'll join me in the coming weeks for discussions on who is hunkier, N'Sync or the Backstreet Boys, and an examination of whether an 11 p.m. curfew is a violation of your human rights.

I promise to bring cookies and donuts.

# Sports jargon to mow down the competition

If I put my game-face on, rise to the occasion, take it to another level and always give 110 percent, I expect to soon be on television.

That may sound strange, but here's the reason for my prediction: Neighborhoods such as mine are now awarding prizes for the best-manicured lawns. This makes lawn maintenance a competition, which of course means it will soon be televised on ESPN and sponsored by Budweiser. It will probably be on after the broadcast of the National Spelling Bee, another bona fide sport.

Whenever the lawn-mowing championships are televised, I know I'm going to have to stay hungry, let the game come to me and avoid a letdown to get my lawn some air time. But I think if I understand my role, make plays, bring my 'A' game and remember that the cream always rises to the top, I can come up with enough sports clichés to mow down interview questions after the competition:

**Q.** That was quite a performance today. What happened out there?

**A.** Well, I knew I had to take it one blade of grass at a time. Early on, I didn't have my head in the game, and I was making a lot of unforced errors with the edger. I was playing not to lose instead of playing to win. And frankly, I went to the well once too often, lost my composure and was so out of sync that I thought I would never get the monkey off my back.

**Q.** Did the comeback start with the trimmer?

**A.** Absolutely. And what can I say about the trimmer? It's a real impact player. It can take over a game, flat-out play and put an opponent on its heels. It's a real go-to tool.

**Q.** What were some of the other keys to your performance?

**A.** Well, it's not just me out there. Remember, there's no I in team, although there are two I's in fertilizer, which has helped defend the home turf. When the fertilizer is performing the way it was today, it really takes the wind out of my opponents' sails. It's like the final nail in the coffin or running into a buzzsaw. They needed a timeout pronto.

**Q.** But you were the leader out there, right?

**A.** Hey, you win as a team and lose as a team. I give all the credit to my teammates, including the mower, trimmer, edger and my two dogs, Casper and Maggie, who helped identify ant hills by barking at them. The dogs really helped the team scratch and claw its way back into the game.

**Q.** It appeared there was some disagreement between Casper and Maggie out there. Can you comment on that?

**A.** That's something I knew the media would harp on, but it's really not an issue. Casper and Maggie are both strong-willed players who want more playing time. And there's only one ball to go around, so there was some bickering. But they're both on the same page and know this team is on a mission.

**Q.** What about some of the weeds that have popped up in the lawn recently?

**A.** Well, my hat's off to them. They have a never-say-die attitude, and they don't rebuild, they reload. I know I can't stop them, I can only hope to contain them.

**Q.** Is this a team of destiny?

**A.** It's way to early to answer that question. But this team is starting to jell and running like a well-oiled machine. Today we were really putting on a clinic out there. But next week we take on another tough opponent, and when we play them, you can throw out the records. We can't relax, because on any given day, any team is capable of beating another team. And we know we can't beat ourselves or let chances to win slip away. But if we give a total team effort, play with heart and emotion during gut-check time, stay mentally tough, get in the zone and maintain our composure, I like our chances. After all, it's not over until its over.

**Q.** And if you win the championship, are you going to Disneyland?

**A.** No way. We can't afford to waste time once the bull's-eye is on our chest. We know everyone else will be gunning for us. We can't rest on our laurels. And most important, the Home Depot is having a sale on fertilizer.

# Halloween is now more trick than treat

The pumpkins are carved, the kids are picking out costumes and the department stores are putting up Christmas displays, so Halloween must be just around the corner.

And isn't Halloween the best holiday? I sure think it is, if you don't count Christmas, Thanksgiving, Easter and National Personal Hygiene Awareness Day.

Long ago I would've rated Halloween much higher. But as the years have passed, Halloween has slid in my ratings, along with jokes about gray hairs and male-pattern baldness. I think it's because I'm now an adult and can no longer trick-or-treat without a written apology for my immaturity.

But each year when kids come to my door to add to their bounty, I remember the fun of Halloween. I remember blitzing the neighborhood for Tootsie Pops, Sugar Daddies and Butterfingers, and the joy of realizing that my prized Milky Way did not have a razor blade in it.

I had to wait for that good news from my parents, who checked my candy to make sure nobody was trying to take the fun out of Halloween. It was a big concern for my parents, but my only concern was that they were taking a commission for their work. Was it simply coincidence that my dad suddenly had a Snickers bar?

My other concern was how aerodynamically sound my costume was. Would it allow me to reach optimal speeds so my Halloween take would be as sweet as possible?

I had reason to worry. One year I was a very cute, but very slow, pumpkin. That was a big mistake. My massive costume tripped me up several times and made running a gourd-awful experience. I slowed my trick-or-treating group down so much that, in a dramatic scene reminiscent of the great war movies, I had to tell the rest of the pack to go on without me.

All the trick-or-treaters in my neighborhood traveled in packs, and we all had the same "take no prisoners" strategy. We trampled through gardens, stomped on sprinkler heads and tracked mud all over as we searched for the holy grail of Halloween treats: full-size candy bars.

Usually we got the miniature candy bars — the ones candy-makers long ago dubbed "fun size." I still don't understand what is so fun about getting a one-bite candy bar or a bag with three whole M&Ms in it.

But each year someone would strike gold, and scream, "The Jones house is giving out full-size Kit Kats!" Immediately, the herd of vampires, werewolves and space creatures would set a trail for the booty.

Today it would be a set of characters from *Pokemon: The Movie*, *Toy Story* or *Chicken Run*, but our outfits 20 years ago weren't that specific. I was usually some ghoul with lots of fake blood, a pair of fangs and occasionally, a football helmet. I wasn't sure what my costume was, but I was sure that I wanted a full-size Kit Kat. And even if I didn't get it, there were enough Sweet Tarts, Milk Duds and Three Musketeers to assure me an aching stomach and a couple of cavities.

Now as an adult, I can only watch the kids in my neighborhood take advantage of Youth Looting Night. Now I'm the one standing at the door, handing out the candy and inspecting my trampled garden the next morning.

But I'm still tempted to join the neighborhood trick-or-treating pack. It's just that a 6-foot-2 guy with fake blood, a pair of fangs and a football helmet probably won't get any treats from the neighbors. Maybe just a visit from the police.

I guess I have to face it. I'm not "fun size" anymore.

# It slices, it dices, it has handlebars

Here's a quick trivia question for sports buffs, people who buff their cars and those who are reading this column in the buff. (Don't try to make any connection, it's just a titillating way to say that this question is for everybody).

What costs more: An Indy racing car or the bicycle American superhero Lance Armstrong rode in the Tour de France?

That's right, it's the Indy car. I know it would've been more dramatic if the bike actually cost more, but even when I added the price of fog lamps, a rear spoiler and a CD player to Lance's superbike, it was cheaper than every Indy car I researched, excluding some of the slower vehicles at Ralph's Go-Kart-O-Rama.

But I can assure you that Lance's bike is no Huffy Roadster. And I can assure you that the price of the bike is astounding. So to ease the blow on any cycling enthusiasts who might want to buy a bike like this, I won't tell you the price just yet. I'll invoke the marketing strategy of Ron Popeil, inventor of the Pocket Fisherman and the wonder product that scrambles an egg inside its shell, who has uttered a million times, "But wait, there's more!"

And believe me, there's much more to this bike than just the standard features, like wheels, pedals, handlebars and a mini license plate that says "LANCE." First of all, the frame of the bike is dimpled like a golf ball, and simple physics tells us why that is an advantage: Any object that is dimpled like a golf ball can be endorsed by Tiger Woods. And we all know Tiger wins everything.

Actually, the dimpling makes the bike more aerodynamic, which is extremely important in cycling. In fact, aerodynamics are to cycling what low IQ levels are to the Beanie Baby industry. That's why all the world-class cyclists wear those egg-shaped helmets, which were probably also invented by Ron Popeil.

So how much would you expect to pay for this bike?

Well, I know you're excited. But wait, there's more.

The aerodynamics are also improved by a tapered seat post, and the bike is three ounces lighter than the previous model. That means Armstrong was able to carry along a King Size bag of M&M's and not feel any more weighed down than last year. That's not to say that any of the Tour riders would actually eat an entire candy bar. These guys are in such great shape, I'm guessing they are strictly a rice cakes-and-protein shakes crowd.

So we've got the dimpled frame, the tapered seat post and the lighter weight, which must impress all of you in the informercial studio audience (APPLAUSE). But once again, there is more. And it's the biggest reason why you'll want to pull out your wallet and make three easy payments for this wonderbike.

The bike includes a revolutionary internal hydration system that stores water within the frame. That's right, WITHIN the bike frame. A straw extending from the middle of the handlebars allowed Armstrong to drink without breaking from his aerodynamic riding position as he dominated the Tour de France. In turn, you'll be able to stay in your aerodynamic riding position as you navigate the challenging Tour de Kroger for a gallon of milk.

It's incredible, I know. And now that the wild applause has died down, I'll get to the price.

Sixty thousand bucks.

That's what it cost to develop and build the bike, which Armstrong rode for just three stages of the 21-stage Tour de France. He rode it only during the time trials because it is not designed for long rides.

But short rides are perfect for you and me, the sports fans who define the longest 15 minutes in life as the 15 minutes on a stationary bike at the YMCA. The sports fans who are stunned that anyone could ride a bike for an entire day, let alone three weeks. The sports fans who are amazed that Armstrong could return from cancer and compete in the Tour de France, let alone win it three straight years.

I admit that the bike is a little expensive. But quality has its price. And just think of yourself cruising down the road, sipping your favorite beverage and knowing that you're at the cutting edge of aerodynamics because of your dimpled frame.

I'm talking about the bike's frame, of course. If your own frame is dimpled, I'd stay away from the spandex biker pants.

# Summer temperatures can give you the chills

As the afternoon sunshine poured through my windshield, a bank sign marked the time and temperature when I went crazy from the heat. It was 6:17 p.m., 96 degrees, and a cow was waving at me.

I squinted my eyes, used my hand to block the glaring sunlight and took another look. A cow, standing on its hind legs, was still waving at me. It seemed to be a sure sign that my head had soaked in too many rays.

Thankfully, I wasn't going crazy. But I'm sure the person wearing the cow suit wasn't feeling thankful. Ninety-six degrees and this poor soul was in a bovine bodysuit, sweating it out as he or she directed me with one hoof to pull into a Chick-Fil-A restaurant.

My guess was that the cow suit was punishment for an employee who arrived late or was caught eating a Big Mac while on the Chick-Fil-A timeclock. Whatever the reason for the sweltering assignment, I assume this was also a talking cow, as in, "Tomorrow I'm going to put in an application at Taco Bell."

Taco Bell might be a good choice, considering getting a person into a Chihuahua costume doesn't seem possible. But my suggestion for the cow impersonator would be a job at a movie theater. I don't know if the money is better or there is an employee discount on the five-dollar bucket of popcorn, but the theater will never be 96 degrees.

It won't be anywhere close. The temperature in movie theaters usually hovers just above freezing, making the room nearly as chilly as the relationship of Tom Cruise and Nicole Kidman. The next time you go to a theater, check out how many people are slowly curling into a fetal position in their seats to battle the onslaught of air conditioning. It's the only defense when you're wearing shorts, a tank top and sandals.

But it's not just movie theaters chilling out in the summer. At many grocery stores, you can feel like you're in the frozen-foods aisle when you're picking out garbage bags. The malls, which will pull out the Christmas decorations in a couple of months, already have a holiday climate. And last week I got goosebumps while waiting in line at the post office.

What's going on? During the summer, does acceptable room temperature drop about 10 degrees?

Office buildings apparently think so. I haven't seen any studies indicating that employees are more productive at lower temperatures, but I hope it's true, because — note to Chick-Fil-A cow impersonator — the temperature is a little chilly where I work at *The Dallas Morning News*. Some of my co-workers even bring jackets to work, and I often take a walk outside in the afternoon to thaw out.

I admit it's a short walk. At 100 degrees, it doesn't take long to appreciate air conditioning. And I certainly do appreciate air conditioning, having grown up in Phoenix, where June to September is pretty much station-to-station living: air-conditioned house to air-conditioned car to air-conditioned office.

I never appreciated air conditioning more than when my wife and I took a summer vacation to Massachusetts two years ago. We spent two hours in a restaurant on Nantucket because it turned out to be the only place on the island with air conditioning. It was far from the most fulfilling two hours of our vacation, but when it's 95 degrees and the humidity is 90 percent, sipping a soda in a cool climate seemed the touristy thing to do.

So no, I can't live without air conditioning. But I can live with a little less of it, especially when the news is buzzing about energy shortages. Raise the temperature a few degrees and maybe we can ease the energy crunch and the indoor chills of summer at the same time.

Until then, I'm going to check my employee handbook's dress code to see if I can wear a cow suit to work.

# Terrorist attack gives Americans new drive

NEAR A SIGN THAT SAYS "AKELA FLATS' FINEST MOCCASINS, EXIT NOW," New Mexico — The billboards along Interstate 10 are putting the hard sell on me. Southwestern jewelry, souvenir panchos and rattlesnake bolo ties are just a few of the items promised at the upcoming gas station/Dairy Queen/gift shop where a coffee mug with my name on it is just $3.99.

Tempting, but I'm not stopping. The gas tank is still half full, and the car is too full to start a collection of Southwestern windchimes. There's no time to stop, anyway, because my wife and I are battling the clock as we drive from Dallas to Phoenix for a wedding.

Yes, I'm really writing this as we make the journey west to our childhood home. I should note that, in an effort to promote safe driving and avoid a rate increase on my auto insurance, I am not writing and driving at the same time. But in the world of high-speed Internet, instantaneous news reports and real-time stock quotes, a real-time column seems to be the next logical step. Of course, this column won't be read until after the trip is over, but that's a technicality that hasn't been worked out yet.

This was supposed to be a column from 25,000 feet in the air — on a flight that would zip us from Dallas to Phoenix in just over two hours. Instead, we are making the 18-hour car ride through Texas, New Mexico and Arizona, passing the time by counting the number of billboards preparing us for "THE THING?"

Here comes billboard number seven: "THE THING? Mystery of the Desert. 123 miles."

Normally, I would be angry about spending so much free time in a car. But after days of cursing the evil that killed so many innocent people at New York's World Trade Center and the Pentagon in Washington, I can't muster any more anger.

Only sadness. Sadness for all the families that lost husbands, wives, mothers and fathers; sadness for all the families who desperately hoped their loved one would be found alive in the rubble; sadness for everyone forced to endure hell on earth.

The terrorists who attacked the World Trade Center and the Pentagon changed America forever. When thousands of innocent lives were lost, we Americans lost the feeling of security within our borders. We lost our feeling of invincibility.

But the terrorists had no idea what Americans would gain: a renewed compassion for their fellow citizens, a swelling of pride, a sense of unity that often accompanies a common wound.

I've never seen this kind of patriotism. Lee Greenwood sings that he's "proud to be an American" on every radio station I find along the trip. Flags flap from the antennas of cars around us, and a paper flag is taped to the back window of a car in front of me. And in the west Texas town of Kent, where there are fewer residents than victims of the recent terrorist attacks, the gas station attendant was wearing a red-white-and-blue shirt that must have been pulled from deep in the drawer. I'm sure it made it over his belly a few years ago.

And looking ahead, I see another billboard: "THE THING? Mystery of the Desert. Nemadji pottery, Southwestern rugs and delicious shakes. 74 miles."

Tacked to the bottom of the billboard is "God Bless America." I never thought a billboard could give me chills.

Just like at Pearl Harbor, an attack on the United States has awoken a sleeping giant. A military response is expected, but that's not the sleeping giant to which I refer. I'm talking about the American people, who for years have taken their country for granted. The Americans who sometimes forget their amazing rights and freedoms as they trudge to work, fight for a parking spot at the mall or complain about gasoline prices.

I'm guilty of that. But I'm awake now, and I won't let my appreciation of this country fade with the news reports of this unbelievable tragedy. I'm even happy that I'm getting to see a thousand or so miles of this wonderful country. Yes, the bathroom in Kent was nearly as infested with germs as the brain of a terrorist, and the absorbency of one motel's towels compared unfavorably with tissue paper. But the beauty of this country, warts and all, amazes me. The lakes, rivers and mountains, the rattlesnake keychains, wallets and shot glasses — in America, they are things of beauty.

But what is THE THING? I'm not sure, and I don't care, because I know the thing that makes this country great. The United States is a place where people of different races, religions and values strive to live together in tolerance, not terrorism.

America is the Beautiful. And through pride, strength and compassion during this sadly unique time in history, I expect America to put it on a billboard for the entire world to see.

# Leaving my job without one sob

Back when I was a paperboy with a delivery that spared no potted plant, I dreamed of doing more in the newspaper business. Instead of breaking ceramic windchimes with a newspaper fastball, I would break stories. Instead of writing notes that read, "Sorry about the newspaper on your roof," I would write headlines.

Now that I work for a newspaper, I should be satisfied with my career. But how can I be satisfied after watching Cowboys quarterback Troy Aikman announce his retirement? How can anyone be satisfied after watching a person, as he *quits* his job, shed more tears than a third-grade class viewing the final 10 minutes of *Old Yeller*?

I can't imagine many people welling up at the thought of retirement.

"I just can't believe it's over, that my day has come," sobbed the retiring manager of Big Al's Hardware. "Monday morning I won't hear the cheery buzz of the 6 a.m. alarm, get dressed, fight traffic and ... I'm sorry, I need a moment to collect myself."

I would only need a moment to collect my things. Maybe a few minutes to pick up my final check and say goodbye to the poor saps who had to keep working. Then I would be off to the career I believe is my true calling: free-time management.

I know my lack of dedication sounds terrible, and yes, I feel guilty about it. At least I felt guilty before talking to T.J. Patida at the megamall near my house.

No, the mall has not added a therapist or spiritual adviser, although both are probably scheduled to be added next to a third Starbucks. Patida is the manager of Candy World, a store in the mall.

Here is the question I posed to her: "If you won the lottery and had enough money to retire, would you keep working?"

There was laughter.

"Not the same job," she said.

So what job?

"Definitely something where I wouldn't work very hard," she said.

That soothed my guilty heart like an upcoming three-day weekend. Now I know that others dream of jobs that don't include timecards, nametags or questions such as "Where do you see yourself in this company in five years?"

Seeking more validation of my work-free vision, I spoke to Mike, an employee of a major fast-food retailer. Mike, who in addition to working a deep fryer seems to have a deep fear of the media, asked me not to reveal his last name or where he works.

But Mike, who I can reveal has worked for the business between three weeks and 14 years and is between the ages of 16 and 42, gave me some very clear responses.

If he won the lottery and had enough money to retire, would he keep working?

There was laughter.

"No way," said Mike, if that really is his name.

You wouldn't work at all?

"No way."

And if you had a news conference announcing your retirement, would there be a lot of tears?

"No way."

How about if during your announcement, you were watching the final 10 minutes of *Old Yeller*?

I didn't ask him that last question, but I'm assuming the answer would be, "No way." That or "Uh ... Are you going to order something?"

Here's my order: One job where I don't work very hard, a side order of being my own boss, and to wash it all down — a super-sized salary that allows me to retire before the rest of my hair falls out. Then I will have a news conference to announce that, although I really enjoy my job, the time has come for me to retire.

I don't know if anyone will show up for the news conference, but I do know this: Either way, I won't shed any tears.

# Time moves fast, so enjoy every sip

When I was working for my high school newspaper, I was well-known for groundbreaking investigative reports such as "MIDNIGHT CURFEW: A violation of your rights?" and "THE SODA MACHINE THAT STEALS YOUR MONEY: Can we stop the madness?"

Actually, I can't take all the credit for those stories. It was the joint effort of a top-notch staff, which was dedicated to exposing the truth, raising awareness and spending two hours in the Burger King parking lot when it was supposed to be delivering newspapers.

Sure, we were just high-school students, but our newspaper wasn't just a school newspaper. We went off campus — and occasionally, past Burger King — to get the scoop. For example, a few of us visited a kindergarten class in 1987 to write a story and take pictures of the students, who were learning the dangers of eating paste and running with scissors. The kindergartners were the high school Class of 2000, after all, so their first day of school was worthy of a 15-inch story and a picture of them learning to sit cross-legged. We thought so, anyway.

The kindergarten story is the one I remember most now, because — allow me a moment for panicked realization that OH MY GOD, WHERE HAVE ALL THE YEARS GONE? I'M GETTING OLD — those kindergartners are now in college. Well, many of them are in college. Others got jobs after high school, some probably joined the military, and if my hometown is the same as when I left, a good number of them dropped out of school and now spend their weekends riding the mechanical bull at a neighborhood bar.

Whatever they are doing, those former kindergartners are part of an elite group. They are the young adults of America, around which modern culture revolves. They are the faces in Gap advertisements, beer commercials (so what if they're not 21) and music videos. They are the authorities on emerging technology, fashion trends and why Puff Daddy changed his name to P. Diddy. They are living in the passing lane and buzzing on Mountain Dew, while my generation, which was king just a few short years ago, is quietly merging into the slow lane and sipping Country Time lemonade.

Hey, I'm not that old. But I am old enough to be jealous. I would love to laugh at hair-club commercials the way I did when my hair was more committed to my head. I would love to be addressed as "dude" or "bud" instead of "sir" or "mister." I would love to not have a portion of my brain that — and I assure you this in unintentional — is counting down the time until my first doctor-recommended prostate exam. I'm cringing right now.

Yes, I'm jealous of the latest MTV generation. But that doesn't mean I want to be them. I didn't want to be a kindergartner when I was in high school, and I wouldn't want to be part of the Class of 2000 now.

There's so much pressure on you. Colleges are getting more competitive and so is the job market. The economy is changing, and crashing, as you size up your future. And just when some of you start feeling smart (you said no to drugs, stayed in school and watched an entire episode of *World News Tonight*), someone says today's young adults aren't very bright. A man, probably sipping Country Time, says he weeps for the future because America's young people are falling behind the rest of the world. He says half of you can't even identify where Iraq is on a map.

Here's a secret, young people: Most Country Time-sipping, slow-lane drivers don't know where Iraq is, either. "Somewhere on one of them continents over there in the desert" is what many would say. And here's another secret: Much of the Country Time crowd still doesn't know what they want to do with their lives. "Not what I am doing right now" would be the common refrain.

Odds are that you'll answer the same way in 15 years. So don't take life too seriously while you're young. You mastered sitting cross-legged, you didn't eat paste and you avoided serious mishaps with the scissors, so you'll make it through life fine.

Take a break and have some Mountain Dew. I think it's best when mixed with a little Country Time.

Printed in the United States
3824